Advance Praise

"*Competitive Advantage* is an essential resource in improving your organization's educational strategy and programs. The book will transform how you create, lead, and deliver education."

Gabriel Eckert, FASAE, CAE

"Presenting immediately actionable ideas, Tracy King has written a book relevant and useful for association professionals on the front-line and C Suite. The first chapter had me benchmarking my own association. Easy to read and understand, regardless of where your association's education fits in the life-cycle, this book will get you thinking and more importantly should inspire you to action. Change can be daunting and King provides tools and a roadmap to help along the journey. Read this book and you've no more excuses. Ready....read...LEAD!"

Greg Fine, CAE, CEO/EVP CCIM Institute

"*Competitive Advantage* fills a significant gap in the association management body of knowledge. It both shifts the continuing education conversation to results, to outcomes, to impact, to providing real value while simultaneously helping the reader build ~~a straight path to execution.~~"

~~...~~AE and Vice President, ~~...~~g, Ohio Society of CPAs

"Yes! ~~...~~ook, Tracy's words turn into discerning Ahas lighting your path to success. This is the must-read book for all association executives and learning professionals. Her insights and depth of value are a gold mine for your reading, reflection and relevant remedies. Tracy sums up her wish and goal for you as a reader in the last sentence of her Introduction: Let's rise together."

Jeff Hurt, DES, Executive Vice President, Education &
Engagement, Velvet Chainsaw Consulting

"This book is a fast, concise set of clear, practical steps organizations can take to evaluate and improve their professional development programming. In a disrupted education-to-employment system, the time to get your overall strategy explicitly defined and bring all of your educational activities into alignment with it is NOW."

Shelly Alcorn, CAE, Principal,
Alcorn Associates Management Consulting

"Conversational and accessible, Tracy has crafted a strategic road map for educational programming success. From the bottom up, *Competitive Advantage: Create Continuing Education that is Profitable, Sustainable and Impactful* clearly defines the alignment of mission, staff and volunteer resources to help busy (think sometimes overwhelmed) association professionals guide their organization to evaluate programs effectively, maximize the market, see opportunities clearly, and scorecard the results in actionable, sustainable ways. A must read for those of us who care and think deeply about the future of workforce development and the role associations play."

Wendy W. Kavanagh, CAE, President, Georgia Society of
Association Executives

"I have been an ED of several associations and have faced many of the challenges cited by Tracy. My only regret is that I did not have the vision and implementation tactics she lays out so well to have helped me address these challenges. This book is a must-read for anyone who sees the value in education strategy versus the hit-or-miss approach so many of us take."

Todd Mann, CAE, President & CEO, Todd Mann
Management Group

"I have struggled to find good resources that speak directly to the current challenges and opportunities within the association education industry. I read this book just before a strategic planning retreat with my education team, and this book really hits the mark! Within the first two pages, I felt like this book was speaking directly to me and the challenges we face in our association. I will be using this book to as a guide to help me work with my team as we create our strategic plan so we can more effectively serve our members. I'm looking forward to moving our learning programs from being transactional to being more transformational."

Kristen Gleason, MA, M.Ed.

"An absolute must read for any organization involved in education. Tracy's no-nonsense approach to laying out the problems faced in education and a roadmap to solutions is insightful, practical and on target. This is not only a great personal read but perfect for teams looking to align and conquer. In your educational capacities if you have ever once wondered what do I do now, this book is for you."

Lynn Rocap, CAE, CMP

"In *Competitive Advantage*, Tracy outlines a tangible road map for associations on how to take the valuable but disparate experts and learning in their midst and transform their efforts into a well thought out holistic strategy that can truly make a difference on the value and experience the organization creates. High-level, tangible, implementable - a must-read for those passionate about learning in associations."

Lowell Aplebaum, CAE, CEO of Vista Cova

"In *Competitive Advantage*, Tracy King builds upon her hard-earned experience gained within the trenches of medical and corporate continuing education to create a road map for navigating the common institutional pitfalls that make the process harder than it needs to be. Her concrete solutions span the entire process from needs assessment to implementation and have proven time and again to be effective and economical. Her prose is lively and engaging, and her analogies, drawn from personal experience, both illustrate her points and entertain the reader. Highest possible recommendation."

Donald Iverson, MD, FAAN, FRSM

Competitive Advantage

Competitive Advantage

Create Continuing Education
That Is Profitable, Sustainable, and Impactful

TRACY KING, CAE

NEW YORK

LONDON • NASHVILLE • MELBOURNE • VANCOUVER

Competitive Advantage

Create Continuing Education That Is Profitable, Sustainable, and Impactful

Published in New York, New York, by Morgan James Publishing in partnership with Difference Press. Morgan James is a trademark of Morgan James, LLC.
www.MorganJamesPublishing.com

ISBN 9781642793680 paperback
ISBN 9781642793697 eBook
ISBN 9781642794410 audiobook
Library of Congress Control Number: 2018913872

Cover and Interior Design by:
Chris Treccani
www.3dogcreative.net

Morgan James is a proud partner of Habitat for Humanity Peninsula and Greater Williamsburg. Partners in building since 2006.

Get involved today! Visit
MorganJamesPublishing.com/giving-back

To my four directions, my four lights,
my four loves, my four seasons
who make me proud every day.

Jordan

Micah

Elissa

Anna

Table of Contents

Introduction

"In the long run, you only hit what you aim at."
HENRY DAVID THOREAU

Lauren settled into her airline seat with a click and slowly released her breath.

Wow, it's been a week!

She was relieved the conference went so smoothly. It had been touch-and-go with Emily suddenly giving notice just before the event, leaving the rest of the staff and volunteers to pick up the pieces and make sure they fit together. Thankfully, the attendees didn't seem to notice how seat-of-the-pants this program was pulled off. Based on immediate feedback, the innovations Lauren introduced really resonated. But she knew this was not sustainable.

She loved her job, but man she was tired.

She scanned her email and text messages to ensure there were no fires to put out on the way home. There always seemed to be something. She was coming up on her third anniversary in this position, and she was frustrated that she could never seem to get out ahead of things. She was constantly making reactive decisions.

She reflexively pressed a knot in her shoulder.

As the plane climbed, Lauren recalled the excitement she had felt stepping into this position. The board had been looking for a leader to take education programming to the next level. She had so many ideas! But she hadn't anticipated the obstacles she'd face–pet programs, sudden board decisions diverting resources away from her projects, team members who were comfortable in their tactical positions and struggled to innovate, the pressure to prove her ideas with revenue before receiving adequate budget to support them.

She realized she needed to pick her battles wisely–making decisions that would render the quickest gains. But then when an idea succeeded, like the innovations executed at this event, she had to figure out how to repeat that success, plus increase the revenue margin. As if it were as simple as a turn of a crank.

Email to self

Subject line: SWOT

Message: Debrief with the team Tuesday when everyone is back in the office to discern what we need to do to make sure this isn't a one-hit wonder.

Lauren reflected on interactions with several members at the event. She loves this industry and the evident passion her volunteer leaders and faculty have for this community. She truly believes in the mission of this organization and has such a heart for this work. But that clutch in her gut reminded her she had to figure out how to jump these ruts. She had to introduce the strategic changes this organization must embrace to really be what it aspires to be for the industry–and stand apart from the competition nipping at its heels.

But how? What next best steps will ensure we get some traction before the target moves again?

View from the Trenches

Feel familiar?

You're in good company here in the trenches. Lauren's story is a composite of the feelings, circumstances, and internal conflict I've encountered in dozens of learning leader clients and colleagues. I've experienced that gut clench myself while serving organizations knowing our reactionary posture was neither sustainable nor the pathway to profit hoped for. But since we don't have unlimited resources to experiment wildly, how can we be assured the choices we make to depart from these norms will give us the returns we need?

The challenging news is there are a lot of association professionals in these trenches and it's easy to stay stuck. It's easier to maintain the rhythm of how things have been operating and grasp for tweaks that may put a little sparkle on it, even though tweaks do not address root issues. Change is challenging, and we're already spread thin. Change requires commitment and coordination through layers of volunteer leaders, staff, and stakeholders. Given the die may not roll in our favor, why invest that effort, even if this pain persists?

The good news is there is a blueprint. Among the possible methods to pivot from a reactionary position to a strategic and intentional one, this is a proven pathway to reliably profitable and sustainable continuing education programs.

You are holding the key to a new future for your organization to make a greater impact on the industry you represent.

What will you do with it?

My career has been devoted to serving organizations in the workforce development trenches. I've served as faculty preparing professionals for the career pipeline. I've served corporations aligning training needs with business objectives to upskill employees for mutual success. And I've served dozens of professional associations intent on remaining the content authority for career development for their industry. Meanwhile I've been a student of the learning sciences, workforce disruptions, learning technology and trends—bringing these insights forward to my clients.

My decades serving the continuing education industry have taught me one thing for sure: the business of continuing education has shifted, requiring a new model for maintaining a competitive advantage.

I've synthesized the culmination of these insights from my career in workforce development into a tool for my clients. Now I'm sharing it with you. Because that clutch you feel in your gut is real. I've felt it too. And I'm passionate about elevating the conversation. The risk of not responding to imminent change is ultimately irrelevance.

I wrote this book because it matters. Because workforce development matters. Because professional associations matter. Because education is intended to be transformational, not transactional. Because we can do better, and I know the way.

Let's rise together.

Chapter 1:
Internal & External Forces

"One thing is for certain: Change."
HERACLITUS

Cascading Failure

It was a gut-wrenching crunching sound. Not good. Cars should never make that noise. My imagination went wild with what the issue may be and how much it would cost me.

It had started out as an occasional squeak in the carriage. I had no problem coming up with reasons to procrastinate taking my Rav4 to the mechanic: stacked work schedule, kids finishing the school year, business trip prep. Also, it probably was nothing and would work itself out, right?

Turns out, I had a cascading failure on my hands.

"A cascading failure is a failure in a system of interconnected parts in which the failure of a part can trigger the failure of successive parts." – Wikipedia

This messy and expensive problem can happen in any type of system: computer networks, bodies, bridges, power grids, and *learning portfolios*.

There's a tendency to hear a squeak and a grind in a learning portfolio, like our annual conference or our eLearning program, and respond with a quick fix we hope will buy us time until we have the resources to really dig in with a good SWOT. That's just like me feeling good about getting routine oil changes but not taking time to find out some factory original parts on my car were busted and causing a mess of other problems not at all associated with where I heard the noise.

Because a system and same-old is not sustainable.

Sure, sometimes we've got a headlight out and just need to change the bulb. Easy. Done. But the squeaks and grinds portend more.

Your learning portfolio is comprised of all the ways members can learn with you: conferences, regional meetings, virtual events, eLearning, mobile learning, textbooks, workbooks, webinars, workshops – whatever you've got that runs on learning objectives. Because of the tendency to manage these programs in siloed teams that do not collaborate or coordinate, we think when we hear a squeak it must be located within that program. We may even do a study on that program or invite a consultant to evaluate it. But when we do not acknowledge that our programs belong to the larger system of learning we offer to our constituents, our quick fix could trigger a cascading failure.

Check it out from this angle: Your members don't see (or care) that different teams support different learning programs within your organization. Your portfolio of learning opportunities culminates within their total experience with your brand. So, if members have a rotten experience with a webinar series package they may share their experience with colleagues and collectively decide not to invest in a new virtual workshop offering hosted by the events team in the same online learning portal. You may see alarming decline in virtual workshop registration. Evaluating your virtual program will not solve that problem.

Another example: Say you're introducing a pop-up talk format at your annual conference but the logistics team is tapped. You pull talent from your eLearning team to fill the gap. But leadership is disappointed a few months later when the online course development schedule is way off track. There's now board pressure to look into what's wrong with the eLearning team. But that's ultimately not the source of the problem.

How do you diagnose your squeaks and grinds?

What the Symptoms Mean

The pain you're feeling is legitimate.

⊙ The board wants new programs, but the budget doesn't support the personnel to fulfill these requests without deep cuts elsewhere (but where?)

- Members are clamoring for on-demand online learning, but selecting and managing that technology feels overwhelming to our already lean team
- Members say they want webinars, but they aren't buying them or attending them if they do register—so do we keep investing in that program?
- The revolving door of leaders passing through our committee and board asking for new things keeps us on the reactive mode hamster wheel
- Our leadership says they want innovation, but implementing change is prohibitive—someone is always unhappy
- We're tweaking so many little things it's hard to know what conditions lead to success or failure—so we can succeed more than throw spaghetti at the wall
- It's challenging to find the time to take a breath long enough to be strategic and intentional with everything going on and all the hats I'm wearing in the organization
- We know we've got work to do to ensure programs are engaging, but where to even begin?
- Registration and revenue are not where we need them to be—and I'm responsible for finding a solution

Quick fixes won't solve these pain points. These are systemic issues, and the diagnostic tool is in your hands.

But first, it's important to understand the context we are operating within.

One Thing Is for Certain

The continuing education (CE) industry is rapidly evolving and increasingly competitive. Let's take a quick scan of the business environment with Strategyzer's[1] four lenses framework.

Market Forces

While each industry will experience pinches due to market shifts, there are several factors that comprehensively impact the continuing education market.

The first is the increasingly complex stratification of market segments. The constituents of our continuing education programs represent a spectrum of groups with diverse wants and needs. Some segments may be growing while others we've long served, and are presently heavily represented in our volunteer leadership, may be in decline. New markets may be emerging, but whether we remain an attractive option for their CE dollars will depend on whether our programs specifically address their needs.

A second market force is the shifting notion of a career. Instead of describing careers as a pathway, we now conceptualize them as "lattices." This allows for multiple entry points in and out of an industry and any variety of lateral, vertical, and diagonal steps to grow within a profession. Describing who fits into early, mid- and advanced career boxes so we can offer meaningful programs and services is more challenging now than ever.

Additionally, the budget pressure our target market segments feel within their own organizations has prompted many professional associations to consider the person possessing the buying power for members as a constituent. To influence buying choices, new communication channels, messages, and sometimes services are warranted for constituents who may never become members themselves.

Finally, the modern learner's expectations have significantly shifted. What they want, when they want it and what they're willing to pay for it requires a new consciousness about the value proposition each of our market segments is looking for.

Key Trends

Trends are tricky. Instead of being The Thing, they are signals of The Thing. For example, microLearning is not a trend. It's a learning format that has been around for a long time. The trend is 24/7 access to educational content at the point of need. And that arises from these key trends that we do need to pay attention to.

1. **Freelance Economy**. Results from Deloitte's *Global Human Capital Trends*[2] report indicate that eight out of ten respondents believe demand for skills is driving a trend toward greater use of contingent workers. And the US is leading the way. A recent report from the US Government Accountability Office[3] estimates that just over 40 percent of the country's workforce is made up of contingent workers and this is expected to grow to 50 percent by 2020. Not all freelancers are full-time independent contractors. Many manage contract work on the side to supplement their income while some seek to gain necessary experience to make

their next career move. *The New York Post*[4] reported one in two millennials have a side hustle. The freelance economy is changing how organizations form teams around tasks, and it's changing how individuals think about themselves as professionals. New types of skills are required to maximize freelance flexibility. Do your education programs address the needs of gig pros in your industry? Or assist leaders with managing talent networks?

2. **Generational Shifts**. The rising and falling tides of generations impact our market segments noted above, but the key trend we need to be concerned about is leadership continuity. While Generation X is amazing and assuming leadership in organizations, there simply aren't enough of us demographically to fill the vacancies boomers will create. Millennials desire to step into leadership well before years of trial and error have chipped off their rough edges. They're hungry for it. How are you helping them prepare? How will the risk inherent in not planning for succession within the leadership team and the promise and pitfalls of multigenerational leadership impact your industry?

3. **Technological Advancement**. Because of technology, the nature of work is changing. How we define a job is changing. How we collaborate with computers–not just use them–is changing with AI on the rise. This not only impacts what training is necessary for our members to thrive, but it has shifted our members' expectations for how they desire to interact with us. For example: If the professionals in your industry are accustomed to using technology every day, they are going to have sophisticated expectations for your learning

management system (LMS). If the younger professionals in your industry are accustomed to both producing and consuming content daily (e.g., YouTube or Snapchat) – and they are – they are going to have expectations for contributing and interacting with you and the content you offer digitally. See how this means we need to step up our game? Also, human skills (once called soft skills) are now in as great of demand by employers as technical skills. The US Chamber of Commerce Foundation[5] has declared a "soft skills gap," calling for a partnership between businesses and educational institutions. How is technological advancement and the resulting skill gaps reflected in your education offerings?

4. **Pace of Change:** I heard a rumor there used to be downtime at work. That we could anticipate busy cycles and slower cycles throughout the year so we could expect the crush of deadlines to even out with the more relaxed times when we could take it easy at work. Anyone experiencing that? Our members feel this pressure as well, learning at the speed of business. And the pace of change within our industries serves up an unrelenting pressure to do more with less which has become a significant driver for on-demand learning. Learning doesn't stop. Learning can't wait for the next event on the calendar or the annual conference next year. Professionals are seeking high-quality resources at the point of need. And if we aren't there, someone else will be. How are you ensuring your learning programs and resources are present at the point of need?

5. **Virtual Workforce.** Work is no longer tethered to a workplace. Virtual teams are on the rise and an increasing

number of professionals expect telecommuting and remote access capabilities. While some point out statistics showing greater productivity from the home office away from workplace distractions, others point out the managerial and logistical challenges associated with a virtual team. Regardless of where you stand on the issue, the variable context of work contributes to the expectation for anytime, anywhere access to learning experiences and resources. We are mobile, so we expect our resources will also be available when we need them, wherever we may be. This trend is borne out by the rise in demand for virtual conferences and asynchronous eLearning. And because we can invite professionals who do not live close to us to join our teams (gig pros or otherwise), that means the professionals we represent are now competing in a global workforce. How will we prepare them?

Consider how each of these trends impact how you function as a business and how each impacts the content and delivery of your learning programs. Also consider the role of socioeconomic trends and regulatory trends that impact your industry specifically.

Industry Forces

If I asked you to pause and list your competitors, how many organizations would make that list?

It's critical to take stock of what the actual competitive landscape looks like. It may be deeper than you anticipated.

The corporate training industry (this excludes associations) is tipping over $160 billion in North America[6]. It represents approximately $360 billion worldwide. The Association for

Talent Development State of the Industry Report[7] indicates approximately 61 percent of this corporate training budget is spent internally on program development, instructional designers, and technology, leaving approximately 39 percent for external services. That's great news, right?

Not when you consider that approximately 26 percent of that external services budget is spent on education corporations, consultants, and licensed content delivered as part of the internal training curriculum. The approximate 13 percent that remains is chiefly spent on tuition reimbursement for MBAs, executive leadership programs, and other formal academic offerings.

Associations are not named as a percentage point in this annual study.

To be fair, associations are lumped into a fraction of the tuition reimbursement category representing *all* credentialing and certificate programs yet not statistically relevant enough to get a pie slice. So that's alarming.

Also consider that academic institutions are keen on growing their pie slice by focusing on for-profit institutional arms offering continuing education courses and certificates. Additionally, a number of corporations and academic institutions have made news with their partnerships on custom training solutions and credentials—pairing the business needs of the corporation with the faculty and learning design talent of reputable academic institutions.

More often when considering our direct competitors, associations list other associations. This is a fact, and it's imperative we mindfully differentiate ourselves from them in ways that are meaningful to our constituencies. They are only the most obvious competitors who should make our list, but by far not the only ones who should hit our radar.

Newer on the market are vendors and publications offering their own conferences and eLearning complete with CE credits. Some corporate LMS subscriptions come loaded with licensed content. It goes without saying that the market for self-initiated learning has exploded. Motivated lifelong learners interested in their options are bound to explore MOOC catalogues and easy access self-serve sources like Udemy and LinkedIn Learning (once Lynda.com).

And since content authority is now evaluated in the eye of the smartphone beholder, associations shouldn't disregard the expert industry. The expert allure is real; in fact, we use it in our conference brochures and eLearning course marketing all the time. But because learning management systems now scale to one (as simple as a WordPress plug in, in fact) rather than restricted to enterprise system scale, anyone can offer professional development to your target audience, and it will sell if the outcome addresses a pain point that prospects seek immediate relief. There is a rapidly expanding market for specific transformation and working with an expert advisor to achieve it.

I think we can agree, given the staggering number of options, learners have to develop their knowledge and skills – it becomes singularly important that we invest in what will set our programs apart and gain the competitive advantage.

Macro-Economic Trends

The global economy may not be your first concern if you're a small regional association, but it should be. It's a grave concern for your members. Whether there's a massive influx of workers for too few jobs or a pipeline that appears to be drying up, whether there's wage inequity in your industry or economic access barriers for your customer's customer, these forces cannot be ignored. Consider global trade, trade wars, and supply chain issues. These are not just advocacy issues, they are education issues. How will you prepare members within your industry to thrive in changing times?

Change is our reality. It's not enough to ride the waves and see where we end up. That's not a sustainable solution. The volume of change in the making requires a deliberate choice.

Solution in Sight

Within each challenge is the seed of the solution–the opportunity to transform challenges into advantages. The root issue may be bigger than you anticipated. It may signal a cascading failure.

When we take time to consider our legitimate pain points alongside external pressures, we can choose to feel overwhelmed and disengage. Perhaps grasp at a duct tape patch to hold the car together for a little while longer. Or we can choose to explore a path forward. We can examine a real fix to the underlying issues and invest in proven solutions.

Do you want duct tape or a real fix?

Those who are interested in a real fix discover unpacking the new value proposition the continuing education market demands is a vital first step.

Chapter 2:

A New Value Proposition

*Value proposition = "The few sentences you need
to dominate your market."*
PETER SANDEEN

The Value Disjunct

Quick quiz: Respond yes or no to the following prompts.

	Yes	No
Is education a component of your association's mission?		
Is education a central value proposition for membership?		
Is your organization interested in extending the reach of its education content?		

Is your association concerned about remaining competitive in your continuing education market?		
Does your association know how to elevate and distinguish your programs from the competition?		

Each time I've offered this poll, the results are nearly identical. At least 95 percent state education is a component of the association's mission, and upward of 99 percent state it's central to the member value proposition. Typically, 97 percent are both interested in extending the reach of their education content but have concerns about remaining competitive in their market.

Despite the extraordinarily high rate of agreement on the first four statements indicating that education is critical to the business's future viability, at least 90 percent *do not* know what to do about it. They agree that their association does not know how to elevate or distinguish programs from the competition.

We've talked about internal symptoms and external market forces. Now let's look at what these mean for your value proposition so we can get at the heart of what will drive your competitive advantage.

Value Shift

Simply having a portfolio of learning options is not enough. For many industries, members *are* interested in a trusted source for earning continuing education credits, but as we've seen in Chapter 1, they have a growing number of options to consider. When professionals are looking at your education programs, they're asking the following questions:

Dear Association,
Why you, why me, why now, why this?
Sincerely,
Your Member

Grab a piece of paper or a notes app and walk through this formula with me.

Why you?

Why should the learner choose you? Why are you uniquely qualified to offer this learning experience? Think broader than the number of years you've been incorporated as an association, which is not, unfortunately, directly correlated to the quality of your learning programs. Hold your target audience in mind and consider how to articulate why they should invest in *your* offerings over your competitors.' Do not assume each of your learner segments knows *why you*. If they did, you probably would not be reading this book.

Why me?

Is it clear to your target constituencies what's in it for them? When articulating your education value proposition, learners will quickly assess whether you're speaking to them directly or spraying the message across a larger crowd. If they cannot quickly determine how a learning experience has been designed to meet their needs, they may assume you're talking to someone else. At the speed of a click, they can easily scan the Google catalog of learning for an opportunity that does speak directly to them.

Why now?

How timely are your program offerings? Are you asking learners to purchase a program now because you are offering it now, or because they *need* it now? Your learners are savvy shoppers, and they will be looking to weigh the benefit of investing time and money now versus later. Your strategic position is this: the right content for the right audience at the right time.

Why this?

Let's assume you've got great answers for why you, why me, and why now. Pick any program in your portfolio—a conference, workshop, course, or webinar—and hold it in your mind. Why should learners invest in *this* program? Dig deeper than the topic. That answer is warm but not quite there. What do your learners value? It's more than a subject, or your programs on topics members have unequivocally stated they "want" would be sold out. What specific need does this program uniquely meet?

If this exercise felt like a struggle, it's because the typical one-size-fits all value proposition is no longer viable when learning consumers are looking for a tailored fit. And when they are in the market to buy learning programs, they're not looking for topics, they are looking for specific results. And so are their employers.

A Pile of Rocks

The truth is, more than not our programs look like a pile of rocks. We create an event. We tell our members: *I'm just going to set this right here. It's a really nice rock and can serve all sorts of potential purposes. Lots of people like you have collected our rocks.*

Members may accumulate a pile of events, but the events are not designed to drive results. They are transactions. Stand-alone experiences. And many of them, despite being marketed as education, are not learning programs at all (see driver 19). This is heartbreaking when you pause to realize you have an entire learning portfolio on your metaphorical worktable that you could coordinate to develop transformational experiences that, step-by-step, culminate in mastery. The results your learners are looking for. The raw ingredients are right in front of you.

But, you may say, our members are different. They're not looking for mastery, they're checking a box. They *have* to take our courses to remain compliant with regulations. That may be true in some cases. But don't you think they will resent compliance training less, and perhaps even become a proud promoter of your programs, if those courses *did* make a meaningful difference within the sequence toward mastery? I'd place that bet.

Learning Is Change

What often happens is we package information in education formats. This a-ha alone is a catalyst that drives conversation deeper with my clients when we are framing their strategy. I see three primary reasons for this result.

1. We do not, as an organization or event team, set different expectations for information programming and learning programming.
2. We primarily rely on industry professionals and speakers who are subject experts but do not know how to design or facilitate learning experiences.
3. We do not presently, on average, hire or contract instructional design talent.

There are exceptions, of course. But only one or two out of every fifty people in conference sessions and workshops I teach say they hire or contract instructional design talent. And few offer training or resources to their subject experts on how to design engaging learning or follow through with the accountability necessary to ensure our expectations are being met.

The result? A rudderless ship. A product produced by consumers with minimal design specifications. An experience out of our hands and out of our control. And the unrelenting pressure to "get better speakers" when the squeak and grind is not necessarily the speaking but the lack of learning design and facilitation.

Now, it's not only fine but at times necessary to offer information-based programs. Conditions change, a new regulation goes into effect, or there's another critical piece of information we need to get in members' hands. This can be accomplished by any number of communication channels, and you may choose to use a session or a webinar, in that instance, as a communication channel. Naturally, the threshold for design is lower because you are just disseminating information. You're informing your audience on a topic. However, that is not learning.

Learning is change

Neurobiologically, when we learn something new, the physical structure of our brain changes. How we think about a subject changes. How we generate new ideas about the knowledge area changes. Our behavior changes. We are able to be or do something different or better.

If you're interested in deepening knowledge, adding nuance to understanding, establishing new skills, developing critical thinking and judgment for better decision-making, and progressing toward mastery, you must design experiences to facilitate change.

But not just any change. A specific change for a specific learner generating their specific desired result.

One size fits all might work for Snuggie®, but it does not work for adult learning.

The New Value Proposition

Information is ubiquitous. It's everywhere. We have more access to information than ever before.

Adult learners don't want to just go to programs; they want to *grow* from programs.

To matter to members, it takes more than offering sessions. It takes improved performance.

Learners are seeking to be or do something different or better. They want deeper understanding, new skills, refined competencies, formative experiences, and peer interaction around content *so that* [fill in your target learner's result]. A few examples:

- Be more efficient to gain back an hour in my day.
- Be an effective leader to a global virtual team.
- Design effective treatment plans for patients with chronic pain.
- Improve financial processes to mitigate risk.
- Become a confident facilitator.
- Deepen understanding of the pharmaceutical options and their interactions to make better choices for patients with a complex diagnosis.
- Survey the features, advantages, and disadvantages of new technologies to make an informed decision for my business.
- Develop the research, writing and copyediting skills necessary to begin freelancing as a medical communicator.
- Explore best practices and a proven process to write grants that win big.

None of these are topics. These examples showcase results: a specific change your learner is invested in. Not mere information about something, but an experience that yields a tangible impact on their day-to-day.

The new value proposition in continuing education is *transformation.*

Transformation is what can set apart your unique value proposition. Your members want to turn to you not for more information from more experts but for your industry authority showing them the way to the results they are seeking. They would love for you to use all of the communication and learning channels in your portfolio to cut through the noise and serve up what's important. They don't want a pile of rocks or disparate pieces of different puzzles. They want you to prepare pathways of learning that guide them toward mastery that impacts their performance and their career growth.

Delivering transformation is key to your competitive advantage.

Learning is vital to the economic survival of the professionals, corporations, and the industries we represent. Distinguishing your organization as a learning leader within your crowded market requires bold moves in a new direction.

To become the irresistible choice within our market, we must commit to a business model that results in transformation.

Old methods will not yield new results for us.

It's time to confront that this isn't an event issue or an eLearning issue or even a program marketing issue. It's an *association management issue.* If education is central to your mission and value proposition, and if you are concerned about your market competition, this is a strategic-level concern.

So much has changed since informational sessions and lectures were added to expos. Back then it was easy to draw a crowd because it was where the professional network convened. If you weren't there, it was difficult to see, be seen, or know what was new and important in the industry. Seismic change has ripped through how professionals network, how they access information, how they want to learn, and the number of options available for each. Just administrating events is no longer the solution that fits the need.

Let's talk about what will.

Strategy to Action Framework

Imagine your future as a learning leader having definitively established your competitive advantage in your market. You've made the transition from reactive to strategic program development. You've built on the legacy of your organization and utilized your resources in new ways to bring solutions to your members' point of need. Your association's programs are no longer just a list of options, but fully realized pathways to career growth and satisfaction. Because of the clarity you've brought to delivering timely information, transformational learning, and meaningful networking, your association enjoys learner loyalty like never before. You are considered the content authority in your industry–the epicenter of meaningful and memorable education that makes a measurable difference. Learners don't just leave your programs feeling good about the content and speakers but are inspired to change, to take action, and to make advancements as a result of the experience you are offering.

Imagine what this shift would feel like and how it would utterly transform your story from the trenches. If you knew there was a pathway to achieving this, would that vision be worth pursuing?

Because there is a pathway. It begins with an evaluation of your system.

Born out of my decades in adult education, I developed a tool for my clients called the Education Enterprise Scorecard. It's composed of twenty-five drivers for developing a profitable and sustainable business around continuing education that makes an intended impact. The drivers are broken out into three segments: Strategy, Portfolio Management, and Learning Design.

What's an Education Enterprise? An organization that builds a business around its education products and services, ensuring it is profitable and sustainable and makes a measurable and intended impact.

Let's quickly overview each.

1. Strategy

Your education strategy should incorporate your organization's overall education objectives, the content domain you are dedicated to delivering on, and your plan for meeting those objectives with your education portfolio.

An effective strategy encompasses all your organization's education programs, and it seeks to position them within the context of their market. Your strategy is ultimately connected to and interdependent with other core organizational strategies, such as operations, communication, and membership.

Purpose: Strategic alignment of business and education objectives governing all learning programs.

2. Portfolio Management

The next segment of the Scorecard examines how you manage your portfolio of programs–whatever mix of in-person, online, mobile, or print options that you offer. This requires we understand the purpose of each education channel in meeting our strategic objectives. When we're managing learning from a portfolio perspective, we can leverage the strength of each program to target the needs we've identified our learner segments are hungry for. We also naturally see opportunities to coordinate programs we're developing into learning pathways so each time a learner finishes an experience, we've identified their next step within our portfolio of offerings. The Portfolio Management Drivers identify opportunities to align talent within our organization with the member experience we want to consistently deliver.

Purpose: Architecting the learning portfolio for efficiencies in content development, deployment, and member experience.

3. Learning Design

The third part of the Scorecard addresses the drivers required to design transformational learning experiences. Designing learning experiences means we utilize the best practices of instructional design for the adult learner when planning any education program. It means each learning event is designed to measure that the learning objectives have been met – that learning is happening. To accomplish this, we design learning for the level of learner that taps relevance and incorporates strategies to help them remember key concepts

Purpose: Producing transformational learning experiences incorporating the best practices of instructional design that are marketable and impactful.

To develop reliably profitable, sustainable, and impactful continuing education, we need to start with your strategy.

Chapter 3:
Education Strategy

"Without strategy, execution is aimless."
MORRIS CHANG, CEO, TMSC

Helicopter View

To celebrate my 40th birthday, we took a four-day Grand Canyon white-water rafting trip. It was life changing!

In the cool of the morning, we helicoptered into the canyon to meet our raft. I could tell the pilot took pride in the *oohs* and *ahhs* he could elicit from passengers as he hoisted us straight up above the ranch where we started our adventure, so we could see where we had been staying in relation to the massive sprawling canyon before us.

Photographs are not worthy of this magnificent place. That didn't stop me from taking hundreds, but realizing I could not behold the entire vista within a single sightline was deeply moving to me. You expect from textbooks and film footage that the canyon is big. *Big* is not even within range of the right word. I was rapt with the expanse of this mighty formation.

With a flourish, the helicopter tipped, and we dipped inside the gape of the canyon, sweeping along the contours and curves of the river. Breathtaking layers of ancient rock loomed above the river rapids. The river seemed tiny until we eased deeper into the canyon to touch down on our beachy landing spot. No, the river was not tiny; we were. The scale of perspective from the sweeping vista to sinking beneath the canyon rim to rafting deep in the canyon witnessing native petroglyphs, hidden grotto waterfalls and the deepest blanket of stars I have ever experienced–I was wonderstruck. It was that feeling you get deep in your chest when there're no words to convey the experience, so you just hold on to the raft ropes and enjoy the ride.

Back home, I reflected on how the contrasting viewpoints of the canyon is a lot like our work. Sometimes we're in the canyon focusing on the rapids ahead of us. We're on-site managing a conference. We're managing several eLearning courses in various stages of development. We're balancing meetings with member calls alongside actual project work on deadline. We just focus on what's immediately in front of us to ride out the rapids.

Sometimes we're helicoptering just inside the rim of the canyon. We can look back and appreciate the accumulation of our efforts. We also can see the bends and turns ahead so we can anticipate taking those corners, charting the best course to meet the challenges ahead. And at other times, we've got the entire vista in view. We survey market trends, what our competitors are doing, and how we can strategically position our organization within the landscape of what's possible.

Coordinating all three viewpoints is critical to bridging strategy to action. The Education Enterprise Scorecard benchmarks your strengths and weaknesses on each these three levels.

Let's begin with the vista view of your strategy.

Strategy Advantage

A comprehensive education strategy guides all education programs–what you deliver, to whom, how, and with what resources. A strategic direction positions your organization's offerings within the broader market landscape, which provides focus on your target so you can measure how close you get to meeting it. Your strategy is a powerful tool for prioritizing and aligning resources, as well as communicating direction to staff and stakeholders.

Unfortunately, a large number of associations don't have an education strategy. According to the 2017 *Association Learning + Technology Report*[8] by Tagoras, 57 percent of the organizations surveyed do not have a formal, documented education strategy governing their learning programs. While nearly 60 percent of associations running continuing education without a strategy is shocking, I suspect the reality is this figure is higher than this sample represents. As Graham Kenny points out in his 2018 *Harvard Business Review* article[9] "Your Strategic Plans Probably Aren't Strategic, or Even Plans," there's widespread confusion about what a strategy is and what it governs.

Our Education Enterprise Scorecard Strategy Drivers will clarify what we need to craft our strategic foundation.

Strategy Drivers

To get the best immediate results from our Scorecard driver discussion, I recommend pulling out the journaling tool you used earlier for the value proposition brainstorm. When a driver resonates with you, capture your ideas (don't wait, they don't usually hang around). Select a time either immediately or later once you've collected a few ideas to reflect on the following:

- ⊙ How could this idea work for me?
- ⊙ What would my desired outcome look like?
- ⊙ Who can help me with this?
- ⊙ What next step will I take?

Now, let's rate your organization on the ten Strategy Drivers, noting opportunities to strengthen your strategic position.

1. Market Intelligence

It's impossible to distinguish yourself within your market when you haven't mapped the terrain. Your strategy begins with positioning your value proposition to win in your marketplace. Your market intelligence should tell you who is buying and selling in your market to help you understand your competition, audiences, evolving needs, and market trends. Your analysis should also produce intel on price points the market will bear to inform your pricing, promotion, and new product valuation. Market insights should be parlayed into your education strategy to accomplish two fundamental things:

- ⊙ Position your programs competitively
- ⊙ Design your programs to meet market needs

You're already naturally collecting a lot of information about your market and feedback from members and program participants. That's a great place to start, but also consider conducting an external market analysis and designing an ongoing listening campaign. Often associations use members as their external market touchstone. Many important insights are born in these stakeholder conversations, but it is best practice to validate these assumptions with market research. A rule of thumb is engaging in formal market research every two to three years, depending on how much your particular market is changing. Any time you plan to introduce a new learning product, conduct a product-specific scan to ensure you're positioning your launch for the greatest success. Continue to monitor your market with an ongoing listening campaign. Your campaign may include comment analysis from program evaluations and any other established feedback mechanisms in addition to a social media listening campaign, periodic focus groups, and stakeholder check-ins. Go where the conversation is happening and benchmark your findings.

Execution Tip: Only collect data that is useful for decision making. Also, only collect data if you are going to *use* it for decision-making. Any time you hand down a request for more data, develop a data plan: how will data be formatted, how will you process the insights and at what intervals for improved data-based decision-making. Make the investment in technology and time to collect data that counts toward intelligence that improves your programs and positioning.

Clients ask me whether they should conduct a market analysis or needs assessment. The answer is it depends on the result you're interested in, as these two different types of studies ask different questions. A market analysis more broadly surveys the marketplace your business is competing within. A market analysis helps a business understand its competitors and customers, informing the business strategy. A needs assessment more specifically researches how your product or service addresses a human need. In continuing education, we're seeking to understand performance gaps, or the distance between the current state and desired results of the learner. Sometimes these are knowledge gaps, and sometimes they're skill gaps. This is much different than asking program participants what "topics" they want to see in future conferences or courses. Once you've identified performance gaps, you can then perform a needs analysis, identifying the root causes of the gap and best methods for addressing it with learning programs. Employing mixed methods to acquiring this information yields richer data for decision making.

This driver asks us to consider whether
- We periodically conduct a market analysis to better understand our competition, our audiences, their

evolving needs, and the pricing the market will bear for our programs and services.

⊙ We parlay market analysis insights into our education strategy to position our programs competitively and align with market needs.

How are we doing?
❏ Red (We're not doing this, or, we've started talking about this, but we haven't done anything about it)
❏ Yellow (We've taken a few steps toward accomplishing this but have work to do to master this driver area)
❏ Green (We're gaining momentum on this, or, we've got a handle on this driver and a plan for what's next)

Action: What insights have I gleaned, and what next steps are necessary?

2. Strategic Objectives

You're up in the helicopter and have a 360-degree view of your Grand Canyon. You've pinpointed your position in this market and articulated your unique value proposition to effectively serve your constituencies. Now how will you make sure you keep that promise to your members and prospects? Craft measurable strategic objectives.

Ask yourself: What are our strategic goals for our learning portfolio?

Your strategic education objectives must guide your overall mission for all education programs and services. Additionally, your objectives must be aligned with the organization's strategic plan and business objectives. We're connecting dots here between your organization's mission, your continuing education market, and the strategic objectives governing your education programs.

"More" is a common generic goal (as in "more registrants" and "more revenue"). While more is typically a good direction, consider ways you can take steps toward the overall result you want for your learning programs. Also, clarify any loose objectives that are framed as hopes and wishes like "to be the industry go-to for x, y, z." That's a vision. Strategic objectives are measurable. We must be able to assess we are making headway toward achieving our objectives.

For my clients who do not have an education strategy and have not yet articulated their strategic objectives, we start by interpreting the organization's mission and vision into its expression for education. How does education fit within the mission and vision, but more so, how do our collective education experiences *contribute* to the organization's mission and vision? From that vantage point, we then identify markers that mean we are fulfilling (or will fulfill) that education mission.

Some of those markers may include:
- Revenue goals
- Market penetration goals
- Global participation, potentially targeting primary regions of focus
- Controlled costs
- Volunteer engagement in education

- ⊙ Professionalizing the industry
- ⊙ Patient safety
- ⊙ Responsiveness to addressing emerging trends in the market
- ⊙ Increasing the number of certified professionals

This is a sample of markers that may become powerful strategic objectives. Notice that by articulating our objectives two important things happen. First, we begin to think about how we will measure our success. (Yes! Hold that thought for driver 10). Second, we realize that each of the programs in our portfolio will have a role to play in achieving these goals. No longer will the annual conference be operating in isolation from webinars and study guides. While each program will have its own unique metrics (which we'll discuss in the Portfolio Management section), every program in the portfolio now must take into account how it will move us forward toward our strategic objectives. Perhaps each will have a role to play in revenue goals, but podcasts will be a mechanism for reaching emerging leaders within your profession and sparking their engagement with your association. Perhaps you'll reserve three sessions at your annual conference to make late-breaking decisions about hot topics to address, but webinars will be a primary source for emerging science, impacts of new regulation, or helping your user group members prepare for new features rolling out, ensuring your portfolio is responsive and nimble to changes important to your learners. Your strategic objectives leverage the expectation that all learning programs will row in the same direction toward your strategic goals. And that powerful momentum will create a competitive advantage for your association.

Execution Tip: If you're not sure where to begin writing a strategic objective statement, draft your ideas in the three columns below and then craft your statement. We will identify the specific actions to support your strategic objectives and metrics within other Scorecard drivers.

Goal	Specific Outcome	Timeframe
Aligned with market intelligence and organization's strategic plan	Clearly stated and measurable; eliminate ambiguity	By when do we expect to achieve this goal

This driver asks us to consider whether

- ⊙ Our strategic education objectives guide our overall programming mission for all education products.
- ⊙ Our strategic education objectives are aligned with the organization's strategic plan and business objectives.

How are we doing?

- ❏ Red (We're not doing this, or, we've started talking about this, but we haven't done anything about it)
- ❏ Yellow (We've taken a few steps toward accomplishing this but have work to do to master this driver area)

❏ Green (We're gaining momentum on this, or, we've got a handle on this driver and a plan for what's next)

Action: *What insights have I gleaned, and what next steps are necessary?*

3. Target Audience(s)

A common error in continuing education is putting together a program for the audience of "everyone." Before the continuing education market evolved to be as diversified and competitive as it is today, organizations could get away with generic programming even though this is not a best practice for learning. This approach is no longer sustainable. Producing a program for everyone is the same as producing a program for no one. If learners cannot identify themselves and their needs in your learning program, they'll find one that does.

It's time to think like Crest. Crest makes toothpaste. Super simple. We all have teeth, so it's reasonable to think we all use the same toothpaste, right? Nope! Crest has invested deeply in understanding its market segments' needs and tooth cleaning experience expectations. They do not pretend to offer one product for all. In fact, you can explore online the more than fifty toothpaste offerings they have specifically crafted for all our tooth cleaning needs. They would not bring a product to market without knowing there's a consumer profile to support it. These are not willy-nilly "I wonder if they'll like sparkles" products. They've done their market research. They have strategic business objectives targeting specific market segments. They know my type: Crest Complete with Scope minty freshening powers, including tartar control and whitening, in a squeezy bottle instead of a big unwieldy tube. How on earth do they know me so well?! When I'm at Cub Foods buying toothpaste and I see that funky shaped bottle in the aisle, I unconsciously register, *This is for me*. Everything about that toothpaste addresses a tooth concern I have and want to solve from the freshness to how the paste is dispensed. They know me and have targeted me in a manner that has earned outright product loyalty. I don't want anything else. Colgate might have something similar in a tube, but that's not for me.

The point is, when your learners receive your program marketing materials or explore your website for learning options, they should experience the same response I do with Crest Complete: *This is for me. This organization knows me. This was designed to help me achieve a result I want. I'm ready to spend my money right now because this is important to me. Thank goodness this organization is tapped in to exactly what I need.*

That's the difference between baking soda (anyone can clean their teeth with that, but why would you?!) and Crest Complete. The audience realizes you see them. You understand them. You have crafted a learning experience with them in mind.

So, does that mean your association must offer fifty conferences for your fifty prospective segments? No, of course not. But it does mean you must understand who your segments are, what they need, and decide who your primary target audience is for each learning experience so they can see themselves in what you offer. The organization who wins the competitive advantage profiles their learner segments and tracks their continuing education needs and preferences. They use that intelligence to design programs to meet those target audience needs. This feels unreasonable only when you're thinking from a particular program's silo. Come down from the silo and survey your learning portfolio array of options.

Consider two practical applications:

- ⊙ We know we have historically attracted students and experienced practitioners to our annual conference. We really want to grow participation by our young professionals segment. How can we attract them to our event?
- ⊙ We've noticed upon auditing our eLearning courses they primarily address pros new to the profession and advanced professionals – leaving a huge gap for midcareer members. How can we craft online learning to meet them where they are in their career development?

The answer to both of these scenarios is understanding your target audience so you can offer programs they will take a look at and say *this is for me*.

Naturally we want to attract many different learner segments as we can to conferences. For large-scale learning experiences we create general information spaces (keynotes, plenaries, forums), but we also must design and market sessions for our primary target learners. Recall learning is not a one-size-fits-all Snuggie® and learners want to affiliate with experiences that were designed to help them meet their desired results. This magic can only happen if you identify your target audiences and leverage that in learning experience design.

This driver asks us to consider whether
- We have defined our learner segments and track their continuing education needs and preferences.
- We design learning programs to meet target audience needs. When they see our programs they respond, "This is for *me.*"

How are we doing?
- ❏ Red (We're not doing this, or, we've started talking about this, but we haven't done anything about it)
- ❏ Yellow (We've taken a few steps toward accomplishing this but have work to do to master this driver area)
- ❏ Green (We're gaining momentum on this, or, we've got a handle on this driver and a plan for what's next)

Action: What insights have I gleaned, and what next steps are necessary?

4. Content Priorities

What are your association's content priorities this year?

If you answered that question with a question, spend some time with me here in this Scorecard driver.

Imagine a world where you're no longer at a loss after a disappointing call for proposals. Imagine working from a content calendar strategically delivering the right content at the right time over the coming year. Imagine not having to scramble to source next month's webinar topic because your content priorities for the year have been established. Imagine the potential of driving content initiatives proactively throughout your entire learning portfolio instead of reactively wedging programs in that a committee member has told us is important.

Identifying your content priorities is necessary for establishing your competitive advantage.

The first step is defining your content domain. Your domain is an outline of subject areas and competencies your organization is committed to delivering upon to support your learner constituencies. Associations in regulated industries like finance, medicine, and law often identify their content domain around the knowledge and skills their members need to maintain certification, licensure, and regulatory compliance so they can practice in the industry. But even outside the clinical topics on a medical recertification exam or the regulation and ethical practice CEs financial advisors need to stay on top of, there are additional requisite skills needed to really excel in one's career. For example, bedside manner, communicating complex legal precedent to a client so they can make a sound decision, or managing ongoing touches with your financial clients on their portfolio goals to maintain your trusted relationship. If these are important to advancing your industry and you're dedicated to providing skill development in these areas, they would be part of your content domain.

Associations in unregulated industries often overextend themselves with a reflexive and unintentional sky-is-the-limit mentality. This stems from not defining their content borders. The topics addressed in learning programs are those that bubble up through committee meetings and call for proposals versus topics identified in advance as critical to the profession. The result: you cannot conceivably measure your content effectiveness when everything is on the table.

By identifying your content borders, what you're committed to delivering upon as an association, you establish the first go/no go of content selection for your programs. Establishing your content domain entails identifying what is critical for your profession—what you will dedicate resources to delivering for whom with your education portfolio. There may be other organizations out there doing better on some subject areas, and you can choose to let them have those areas or do it differently for different target audiences by the line you draw. It's OK to not do it all. Please realize it's better to select what you want to master for your industry over delivering broadly with mediocrity.

Think about it as your content sandbox. Within your sandbox are all the sand buckets of important knowledge and skill areas you want to support with your education portfolio. Anything outside the sandbox is not priority. You can still offer a session on one of those areas, but you will dedicate resources to ensuring your content sandbox is covered before diverting resources to boutique projects—strategically aligning priorities with resources.

Once you've identified your sandbox, note content priorities within that domain for the coming year. Some of those content areas will be fundamental and covered by ongoing programming. Others will clearly need additional attention because they address a pressing need, a critical gap, a new learner segment, or emerging science that professionals in your industry need. These priorities can now be strategically delivered throughout your portfolio over the next budget year, or duration of time you determine, to address these learning urgencies.

Notice the strategic power in identifying your content priorities. No longer are you starting with a blank slate and asking the void who can speak and what do they want to talk about in your next call for proposals. Your content priorities meet specific needs of your target leaners and roll up to supporting your strategic objectives. Your content priorities give the learning programs in your portfolio "assignments" for the year to comprehensively address the priority needs you've identified within your industry. Content priorities drive the types of learning experiences you will offer to fill those gaps, ensuring the programs you do develop make a meaningful and measurable impact. Identifying your content priorities allows you to align resources with what's important, ensuring talent, volunteer time and credit hours are dedicated to the priorities of your industry instead of dictated by the results of a call for proposals.

This driver asks us to consider whether

- ⊙ We have defined our content domain – an outline of the topics our organization is committed to delivering to support our learner constituencies.
- ⊙ We have noted our content priorities within our content domain for the coming year to guide the development of learning programs.

How are we doing?

- ❏ Red (We're not doing this, or, we've started talking about this, but we haven't done anything about it)
- ❏ Yellow (We've taken a few steps toward accomplishing this but have work to do to master this driver area)
- ❏ Green (We're gaining momentum on this, or, we've got a handle on this driver and a plan for what's next)

Action: What insights have I gleaned, and what next steps are necessary?

5. Program Pricing

How does your organization establish learning program pricing? Best practice is defining consistent pricing, discounting and refunding procedures for all education products, and transparently communicating pricing and procedures to your constituencies. Let's unpack.

The first question many of my clients ask is "what should we charge for x?" There isn't a set best price for a conference, webinar or online course, so let's set that question aside for a moment and address some fundamentals that will help us answer that question.

Does your organization have a pricing rationale? Your pricing rationale should be based on your market research, your organization's average dollars per credit hour, the perceived value of the education offering result, size of the market for this offering and market demand. Based on those criteria you can develop a formula for competitively pricing your programs.

From there, consider discounting as a strategy versus a fire sale of "unwanted" goods. Desperate promotions can instruct your members to wait it out for the prospect of deep discounts over purchasing programs at normal market rates, undercutting your value proposition and prospective revenue. Employ promotions for strategic purposes such as attracting a new target audience to a learning program, enticing learners to try a new format you're introducing, or investing in a program bundle at a great rate that doesn't gut your budget.

And don't neglect to articulate your refund procedures. I often see flagship programs have fully fledged pricing structures, policies, and internal processing procedures while other programs, we'll just say eLearning, is case-by-case, seat-of-the-pants, see-what-surfaces. Now that we're interested in cultivating our competitive advantage, it's important we invest in consistent policies and processes for all learning programs despite their tenure with our organization. Establishing policies kindly communicates to consumers and staff administrating programs under what circumstances refunds are eligible and when they are not.

These polices then trigger workflows to process requests timely and efficiently. If we do not invest in at least drafting a framework for our policies and procedures, we can expect staff will receive requests and spend unanticipated time searching for the correct answers on a case-by-case basis when we could have defined this from the start. If you want to achieve business results, you've got to function like a business. This doesn't mean we're a harsh, unfeeling, transactional business that cannot relate to members' woes of registering as a nonmember unintentionally. It means you establish a framework within which exceptions may be made instead of allowing an exception-based universe to dominate your staff's day at the office seeking levels of approval for each request. I guarantee you've got other things in mind for their time.

Execution Tip: If the best approach to the pricing question remains in your mind, here are additional guidelines.

1. Align pricing with your budget and strategy
- Consider your revenue expectations for the program.
- Consider whether this program must fund itself or is subsidized by other funding sources in your business model.

2. Market
- Pricing should consider what your target market will bear.

⊙ Establish where your offering lies within the spectrum of similar offerings provided for your target market.

⊙ Consider what your organization's price per credit hour range is across in-person and current online programs.

⊙ Consider whether you will accommodate pricing barriers for particular global regions.

3. Profit Margin

⊙ Factor in development costs, course media development, and design.

⊙ Decide what an acceptable profit margin is for your programs from a budgetary perspective.

⊙ Some organizations require a profit margin that covers development costs; some organizations subsidize pilot events or eLearning with other programs and are less concerned about the margin factor.

4. Perceived Value

⊙ Consider the content quality, timeliness, and specificity. General education (aiming to reach the widest possible audience versus the needs of a target learner), courses composed of repurposed or curated resources, and courses that do not relate to a cycle in the industry or threshold in career development are considered lower value—requiring a lower price point.

⊙ Well-designed professionally produced learning experiences featuring qualified subject matter experts (SMEs) and directed toward a specific audience and need are considered higher value–and fetch higher price points.

- For eLearning, the level of interaction impacts perceived value. Higher levels of interactivity are priced higher. Courses featuring personalized feedback or interaction with an industry expert are priced even higher.

5. Anticipated Volume

- Given the total market, your current penetration, and your expected market penetration, what anticipated volume do you expect for learning programs? Depending on your answer, consider your pricing strategy based on prospective volume. For example: Is our goal to sell fewer courses at a higher price point? Is our goal to sell many courses at a lower price point?

- Consider whether and how you intend to discount in the future so discounting doesn't promote a "coupon culture" expectation that cripples your earning potential.

This driver asks us to consider whether

- We have defined consistent pricing, discounting, and refunding procedures for all education products.

- We communicate our pricing and procedures clearly to our constituencies (i.e., they don't have to search to find this information; we are transparent)

- Promotions and discounts serve a strategic purpose.

How are we doing?
- ❏ Red (We're not doing this, or, we've started talking about this, but we haven't done anything about it)
- ❏ Yellow (We've taken a few steps toward accomplishing this but have work to do to master this driver area)
- ❏ Green (We're gaining momentum on this, or, we've got a handle on this driver and a plan for what's next)

Action: What insights have I gleaned, and what next steps are necessary?

6. Technology Infrastructure

This driver asks us to evaluate the effectiveness of our technology infrastructure through three lenses.

First, ask yourself: Does our tech infrastructure support the coordinated delivery of our programs allowing cross-program collaboration and program development efficiencies.

This lens asks us to survey internally noting whether our technologies support efficiency or introduce obstacles to collaboration. One example: Naturally, teams develop around events and learning programs. But when technology and workflows bind us within silos, there are redundancies in program management and barriers to developing program synergies. For example, all your learning programs recruit subject experts and collect data on their performance. Some of that data is evaluation data and some of it is internal administrative data, such as when a speaker doesn't care about deadlines or when a subject expert is a great writer but isn't the greatest host for a webinar.

What if, because you have now identified your content priorities for the year and which programs will address them, you coordinate faculty recruitment? If your technology allows learning program teams to share this intel and collaborate throughout the year, you will know which experts are being tapped too hard, which experts bring the house down on particular subject areas, and which may need additional support from the team to execute on a project. Equally important to consider are conflict of interest forms; are you asking faculty to fill them out for each individual content volunteer opportunity they accept or are you governing COI across products, so your faculty aren't completing a redundant step? Or consider content development coordination; are learning objectives for your programs this year tucked away in spreadsheets distributed among an array of local folders, or are they visible and accessible in a SharePoint site so programs can coordinate and promote next step opportunities? Your tech infrastructure should pave the way to greater collaboration among your programs.

Second, ask yourself: Does our tech infrastructure standardize the member experience across programs?

Each time a member logs on to your site, registers for a program, or reaches out with a question or for technical assistance, that's an experience with your brand. Your tech infrastructure should be designed to support the intended experience. For example, whenever possible, offer single-sign on (SSO) so members don't have to generate and remember passwords for your website, annual conference registration site, LMS portal, and publication app. Whenever possible, standardize the registration experience for your learning programs. If different registration technologies are required, how can you align the workflows to reduce confusion and improve the experience? Whenever possible, standardize your "steps-to-help" so that one program doesn't require a form that sits in a queue while another program gets the direct desk number of a staff member. Maximize your technologies to manage a seamless experience for members and member prospects.

Third, ask yourself: Do we select and implement technology solutions that strategically meet our business and user experience objectives? This includes both in-person and digital learning opportunities.

This lens asks us to establish our requirements for technology so we can collaborate with our vendor partners on satisfying solutions. *Requirements* is a technical term that essentially means we have given thought to use cases for our customer and tech administrators, so we know exactly how we need the technology to function to achieve an experience. When you purchase QuickBooks off the shelf at Best Buy, you get what you get. When you're working with a technology partner for your LMS, AMS, networked office, etc. – these are all the things they want to know about your needs, so they can demonstrate how their product fits your desired solution. Requirements are a tech vendor's love language; get to know it! If you don't want to learn this language, hire a consultant to translate because this is critical to your partnership and to your long-term happiness with the implementation of your technology choices. Define your technical, functional, user experience, and administrative requirements. All of these should align with your business requirements. This is how we roadmap our technology infrastructure to maximize capabilities and efficiencies.

This driver asks us to consider whether
- ◉ Our tech infrastructure supports the coordinated delivery of our programs allowing cross-program collaboration and program development efficiencies.
- ◉ Our tech infrastructure standardizes the user experience across programs.
- ◉ We invest in technologies for live and digital learning that strategically met our business, program, and user experience objectives.

How are we doing?
- ❏ Red (We're not doing this, or, we've started talking about this, but we haven't done anything about it)
- ❏ Yellow (We've taken a few steps toward accomplishing this but have work to do to master this driver area)
- ❏ Green (We're gaining momentum on this, or, we've got a handle on this driver and a plan for what's next)

Action: What insights have I gleaned, and what next steps are necessary?

7. Internal Partnerships

If we want education programs to drive membership, if we want our publications to promote and extend the conversation of content priorities, if we want the communications team to creatively market programs using our channels to effectively reach out different learner segments – we have to design staff structures to facilitate collaboration. Silos within an organization are not the way things are, they're the way we allow them to be. Silos are not a product of organizing teams and posting org charts. They are a result of the culture and processes that permit them to exist. To master this driver, your team structures and processes must reflect the integral nature of internal partnerships in shared success.

Imagine a future where your education and membership teams collaborate on shared success. Membership packets and prospect outreach accurately reflect the unique value proposition of the programs within your portfolio for the professional receiving these materials. Program pricing and promotions are coordinated to drive renewals and entice growth in a member segment you're strategically seeking to grow. Frequently asked questions in the call center are communicated regularly to the education program teams so root causes can be addressed. The education team organizes training on new programs launching or new event features. This way the call team can confidently answer incoming questions. Greater continuity of the member experience flourishes with improved communication between the education team and member services.

Or imagine communication team members participating in every event kickoff so they can begin building a marketing plan from the beginning of the process when event objectives and new features are being formulated. Based on the other initiatives the marketing pros are working on, they may be able to recommend synergies that can both increase the value of outreach and reduce the number of emails sent to members each week. Consider the power of the eLearning team and communication team sitting down together quarterly to discuss the development calendar together for future promotions and review data correlating marketing with course registration over the past term so you can have an informed conversation about messaging strategy.

All of this and more are possible when your education strategy is interlaced with other core organization centers, including operations, membership, publications, website, advocacy, etc., prioritizing internal partnerships to achieve strategic goals. Internal partnerships improve the quality of the member experience and efficiency with which it's delivered. Internal partnerships are also critical to the effective management of the learning portfolio, which we will discuss more in Chapter 5.

This driver asks us to consider whether
- Our education strategy is interlaced with other core organizational centers including operations, membership, publications, communications, website, etc.
- Our team structures and processes reflect the integral nature of these partnerships in shared success.

How are we doing?
- ❏ Red (We're not doing this, or, we've started talking about this, but we haven't done anything about it)

❏ Yellow (We've taken a few steps toward accomplishing this but have work to do to master this driver area)
❏ Green (We're gaining momentum on this, or, we've got a handle on this driver and a plan for what's next)

Action: *What insights have I gleaned, and what next steps are necessary?*

8. External Partnerships

One of the greatest concerns I hear from learning pros in the association trenches is the pressure to do more when they already feel spread so thin they're threadbare. The complexity of the continuing education market and the wide variety of learning needs among our audience segments should trigger realization that we can expand our capacity, and our reach, with external partnerships.

While there's no prescribed number or types of partnerships ideal for every organization, your strategic objectives may point toward a combination that would be suitable for yours. Let's look at a few options to consider.

Content Affiliates: Upon examining your content sandbox and content competitors, you may note there are organizations you could partner with to coordinate program efforts. These may be other associations, education corporations, consultants, or your chapters. How can you extend your reach while inviting additional helping hands?

Academic Institutions: If the worker pipeline is a concern for your industry, consider collaborative curriculum partnerships with academic institutions. Produce a trade curriculum for high schools that results in a certificate employers will recognize and prioritize candidates for their entry level positions. Collaborate on a career transition curriculum for your industry delivered through the continuing education arm of colleges near concentrations of employers. Partner on a competency-based assessment built on a college curriculum that offers third-party validation that the appropriate level of skill was mastered. Broker internships with your trade members and the academic programs preparing the future of their workforce. Decide not to live in a vacuum and forge collaborative partnerships with academic institutions.

Corporate Training: Corporations with and without training departments license training from external organizations for skill building and leadership development in alignment with their business objectives. Not only should we as professional associations be asking corporations what skills they're looking for when hiring so we can address those needs in our programs, we should be seeking to develop content partnerships – employers licensing learning experiences to get our expertise and industry best practices within the walls of internal training. These learning experiences can be turnkey skill-building workshops, a customized portal with our eLearning content, or even customized premium experiences delivered by our industry subject experts. Develop relationships with the HR Directors and Chief Learning Officers in your industry to see how your content can supplement training they are offering while generating a robust new revenue stream for your association.

Other key partnerships that need our nurturing are vendor, sponsorship, and volunteer relationships. We cannot do what we do without these important collaborators. Often, instead of thoughtful partnerships, I see transactional dealings. Let's consider a few ways to improve these relationships.

Vendor Partnerships: Your vendors should be interested in getting married with your organization. If they're not equipped for a long-term commitment and the health of your relationship, they're probably not a good fit. Similarly, it's important for you to view your vendors as partners as well. Considering education technology vendors as an example; your LMS partner likely has compiled extensive administrator documentation, courses, and update webinars to assist you in building the best learning experiences possible with their software. Read the documentation. Take the training. Coordinate quarterly calls to talk about how things are going, what features you would like to see, and what's on their tech development road map. They want to know you and your needs. Think of them as a partner versus just a service provider. Also consider vendor offers to off-load your staff with technical support or learning design support. If you don't have these capabilities within your team, consider how partnering could improve your learner's experience.

Sponsorship Relationships: Our beloved sponsors help make education programs possible. But they too are not interested in a Snuggie® approach. Just because we offer a sponsorship opportunity does not mean that option is attractive. Our sponsors are businesses. They have their own business objectives. Their participation underwriting programs must serve a value proposition that advances your objectives as well as theirs. Having a booth is not the thing. Face time with your members may be the thing, but there may be alternative and more effective ways to do that in conjunction with a booth that are valuable to your sponsors' goals. Get to know them. Build a relationship with them. Understand where your mutual value resides.

Member Stakeholder and Committee Partnerships: We don't often think about member stakeholders, our education committee, or program subcommittees as external partners. I introduce them here as part of this conversation because while member leaders are not making business decisions for the association, they have incredible influence. Consider how you are intentionally crafting the stakeholder group experience to be a meaningful contribution in service of your strategic objectives. What is their charter? What goals is each group working toward? How can we measure success, outside of registration numbers and revenue, which are often not indicators for them about their volunteer work? Note opportunities to align volunteer contributions with your objectives for the learning portfolio. Clarifying roles and measuring results translates into a meaningful member contribution. We volunteer for organizations we believe in to make a difference. Help them help you.

Seek out the powerful mutual value you can forge with your external partners. Tap new corners of the market by realizing your incredible partner opportunities that can not only drive significant passive revenue, but help you achieve shared strategic workforce development goals effectively and efficiently.

This driver asks us to consider whether

⊙ We maximize external partnerships to achieve our objectives and mutual value.

⊙ We cultivate collaborative partnerships with our volunteer stakeholders that maximize their meaningful contributions.

How are we doing?

❏ Red (We're not doing this, or, we've started talking about this, but we haven't done anything about it)

❏ Yellow (We've taken a few steps toward accomplishing this but have work to do to master this driver area)

❏ Green (We're gaining momentum on this, or, we've got a handle on this driver and a plan for what's next)

Action: What insights have I gleaned, and what next steps are necessary?

9. Resource Allocation

Quick question: Is your budget an expression of your strategic priorities?

Here's another one: Does overhead, such as staff and volunteer time allocation, align with your strategic priorities?

If I could step into your organization and upon scanning your budget allocations and timesheet cost-centers reverse engineer your strategic priorities, you're in good shape. Alternatively stated: We can't call something a strategic priority if we don't assign adequate resources to it.

Resource allocation isn't something that happens once a year when we're budgeting. It's an ongoing dance balancing time, money, assets, and talent in service of what's presently important. We naturally support our competitive advantage by clearly articulating how we will assign appropriate resources to what we've decided is important.

To measure your organization on this driver, ask yourself

- Does our organization commit an appropriate level of resources in terms of talent, technology and development costs for education programs?
- Do we have processes to openly communicate about insufficiencies, mitigate issues, and align priorities with resources?
- When unexpected opportunities arise that we decide as an organization to act on, do we have a mechanism for measuring talent capability and capacity and shifting priorities so our team is supported in taking on new projects?

Commonly after presenting a conference session, at least one learning pro on the front lines of executing a program (typically webinars or eLearning) will approach me and say something like this: *I hear everything you're saying and agree that's exactly what we need to do to elevate the quality and impact of our online programs. But our board [or committee or my supervisor] decided we need to produce two events a month in our recent budget. I'm the only one working on these programs so I'm just trying to survive — there's no bandwidth for thoughtful*

design or speaker collaboration or even any sort of strategy other
than more webinars and more registrants (which I feel like I
have no control over). How do I help them realize this is not
sustainable? I feel like I'm failing.

These are your staff members. They're telling me a budget
was created in a room with no real understanding for the
resources required to fulfill delivery. And they're telling me
they feel helpless. There's no outlet for an open conversation
to achieve appropriate alignment. They also feel like they
are failing you and the members you serve. Which feels
terrible. Let's agree this should not happen. While I realize
"doing more with less" is a typical slogan within association
management, that's not what this is. This is misalignment.
This is asking for loaves-and-fishes miracles. Not only will
the results be unsatisfying to program participants, but
you stand to lose talented staff as well. It's imperative that
when we set our strategic objectives, we assign the necessary
resources to support the outcomes we seek. It's imperative we
align talent with our priorities. And while we're at it, develop
safe and productive outlets for communication to ensure
we're all rowing together toward our shared success.

To maintain a competitive advantage, your budget
should not only be concerned with controlling expenses and
producing revenue but also about alignment.

How are we doing?
❏ Red (We're not doing this, or, we've started talking
about this, but we haven't done anything about it)

❏ Yellow (We've taken a few steps toward accomplishing this but have work to do to master this driver area)

❏ Green (We're gaining momentum on this, or, we've got a handle on this driver and a plan for what's next)

Action: *What insights have I gleaned, and what next steps are necessary?*

10. Evaluation Strategy

The final driver in the strategy section of the Education Enterprise Scorecard is crafting an evaluation strategy. This driver asks us to articulate measurements for our strategic objectives (driver 2) and implement a dashboard for tracking our progress. If we don't know what we're aiming for, how will we know when we've hit the mark? If our staff doesn't know what concrete role they play in reaching our strategic objectives, and work is not measured against it, chances are they will formulate their own goals and objectives. That means resources are being spent on side trips you didn't intend to buy. Your shared destination must be clear and must be measured (i.e., accountability) to ensure you get from DC to Minneapolis without a wide swing through St. Louis first.

Consider your metrics the GPS for your education portfolio that keeps everyone on the path toward executing your strategic objectives. To make your metrics work for you, develop a plan for pulling data at critical intervals to notice trends and prepare for decision-making.

Benchmark this driver by rating your organization on the following

- ⊙ We track metrics across education programs, products, and services, measuring the success of our strategic objectives.
- ⊙ We maintain a dashboard for these metrics so we can spot trends, intervene as issues arise, make informed decisions, and report accurately to the board.

How are we doing?
- ❏ Red (We're not doing this, or, we've started talking about this, but we haven't done anything about it)
- ❏ Yellow (We've taken a few steps toward accomplishing this but have work to do to master this driver area)
- ❏ Green (We're gaining momentum on this, or, we've got a handle on this driver and a plan for what's next)

Action: What insights have I gleaned, and what next steps are necessary?

If these drivers feel massive and overwhelming and, well, just not tangible enough, you're likely similar to the tactical leaders I've coached. These leaders like the doing. They enjoy riding the rapids and the immediate feedback executing each raft swivel around the jutting boulders in the river. And while the rapids are exciting, we'll never get where we're intending to go without this strategy foundation. These drivers compose key decisions we must make to set our course. Our decisions comprise our pathway–different decisions would require a different tactical route. The effort to wrestle with these decisions is worth it. With your clarity of purpose and direction, your strategy is now rooted in intention.

REFLECTION

- ⊙ Review your ratings for each driver. Which are of highest concern?
- ⊙ If the Strategic Objectives driver is rated red or yellow, what next step(s) will you commit to establishing this critical foundation for your organization?
- ⊙ What opportunities for alignment with your strategic objectives do you notice that could produce some quick wins for your association?

Chapter 4:
Setting Your Strategic Foundation

"Strategy has little value until it's implemented."
BRIGHTLINE INITIATIVE

The Strategy Drivers of the Education Enterprise Scorecard alone are not your education strategy. They are a foundation of choices that inform the development of your strategy. Defining your market position, strategic objectives, and the who/what of what you intend to offer prepares you to design the "how" of your education strategy. Naturally, an education strategy will incorporate the other drivers as well as connect with other strategies within your organization such as certification and membership.

But what happens if you just say, nah, and decide not to develop an education strategy?

First, that's a bold move I can't get behind. But if we must, here's what happens.

Lost profit. Organizations that don't properly position within their market don't establish a value proposition that cuts through the competition noise to sustain revenue growth. More emails aren't what it takes. These organizations often price their programs poorly, some too high and out of range for their targets, and some too low, leaving money on the table. Essentially, the market passes them by and they are unaware.

Lost momentum. Picture yourself in the raft on the Colorado River with team members on each side digging hard at the water rowing in different directions. How far and in what direction would you go? Without measurable strategic objectives there's no target to aim for or an opportunity to celebrate a bull's-eye. When goals are unclear, unmeasurable, and unattended in a PowerPoint deck that becomes a hazy memory once it's closed after the presentation, organizations can't expect to make real progress. And again, the market does not pause for us to catch up.

Lost interest. Organizations who identify their target audiences for programs can then design learning experiences that spark interest, generating registrations. Because those audience segments say *this is for me*. Programs that are for everyone are for no one. Even Snuggie® has target audiences that impact its design choices and marketing decisions! If your market doesn't identify with what you're offering, they will lose interest.

Technology barriers. Organizations that put patches on their tech infrastructure and expect staff to maintain work-arounds instead of investing in developing appropriate solutions create barriers to team collaboration (reinforcing silos), to process efficiencies (so much redundant work), and to data (no data lake for you!). All these negatively impact the member experience.

Missed partnership opportunities. Organizations that aren't strategic and intentional about partnerships miss a lot of great opportunities they won't encounter otherwise. And by grabbing any partnership invite that comes along, organizations risk making commitments that are not in alignment with where they want to go.

Misused resources. Organizations that don't align resources with strategic objectives waste money, time, and talent.

Red Light, Green Light

If you rated your organization green on the Strategy Drivers, congratulations! Amazing work! You're ahead of the curve and likely here to polish an already highly functioning learning portfolio.

If you rated your organization yellow on the drivers, pause to appreciate your progress and the effort taken to lean in the right direction. Really well done. Some common misfires I see with organizations in the yellow zone include:

- ⊙ Objectives aren't measurable. Ambiguous objectives mean we don't have to deliver any bad news about not measuring up but also means we are not really aiming for anything. Arrows flying all over the place.
- ⊙ Sketchy implementation plan. When we don't define tactics, assign responsible parties and are weak on metric follow up, it's difficult to get any traction.
- ⊙ Lack of alignment. Priorities and resources must align or we're setting ourselves up for failure. This

also happens when we assign the wrong talent to implement tactics.

⊙ Follow through fail. When change feels challenging (or a VIP member is loudly opposed to something new we're trying) and we allow that to derail our follow through, we buckle ourselves into the yellow zone hamster wheel where we only talk about change; we don't actually do it. All of these are avoidable and fixable. And that's great news.

If you rated your organization red for most of the Strategy Drivers, don't despair. Many of our clients have started out right where you are and we've worked together to quickly put these pieces in place so they can gather momentum around their immediate priorities. You now have a framework for digging in and talking points to start those conversations. Commit to setting your strategic foundation and dig in.

Your Competitive Advantage

These drivers request top-down commitment–leadership in alignment with execution. Our purpose with this segment of the Scorecard is strategic alignment of business and education objectives governing all learning programs. With our target in sight and the alignment of resources, talent and partnerships fueling our momentum, we can earn our competitive advantage.

Now let's explore what gains we can make by operating with a portfolio perspective.

Chapter 5:
Portfolio Perspective

"The world changes when we change our perspective."
JENNIFER WILLIAMSON, AIM HAPPY

Resetting Our Default

It's easy to see how the current structure of many associations harkens back to their grassroots days when industry pros formed committees to put programs together. Committees are typically insular and task focused, given that volunteers have a limited amount of time to dedicate to a project. Strategic planning often happened elsewhere while committees put execution boots on the ground. Committees consult agendas of previous years to build a program and administrate the event. A vast majority of associations now have staff to produce learning programs, but we haven't much departed from this pattern.

Here's what I notice:

- Staff teams have grown around administering programs and do not, out of process, collaborate with other programs.

- Staff on different program teams complete many of the same process steps, yet do not share intelligence with one another to build efficiencies into program development, subject expert recruitment, centralized conflict of interest processing, standardizing core evaluation questions, etc., resulting in a lot of duplicative work and overtapped experts.

- Conferences don't know what webinars are presenting, webinars have no idea what the publication is covering, workshops and eLearning have no way of knowing what the other is preparing. Potential synergies are lost. And members' experience with your brand and with your content is disjointed and variable.

- We hire staff to administrate events, and our processes and culture bind them to their silos even when we declare we want to see innovation and collaboration. We may be able to produce a one-off collaborative effort, but it doesn't "stick."

These often unintentional structures have become intentional means of doing business. And they *reduce* profitability, sustainability, and impact.

The alternative is to widen our lens and adopt a portfolio perspective. Just as each of the divisions in your organization has a role to play in your strategic plan, each program within your learning portfolio should be assigned a role to play in achieving your education strategy.

Your portfolio perspective is like that helicopter dipping into the rim of the Grand Canyon, surveying the bends ahead and strategizing how each learning opportunity you offer members will help your association realize its objectives.

So, let's take a look at the eight Portfolio Management Drivers and consider decisions and key efficiencies for managing education programs.

Portfolio Management Drivers

Open your journal again and rate your organization on the next set of drivers, keying in on opportunities for efficiency and sustainability.

11. Business Plan

To become reliably profitable and sustainable, you have to operate as a business, meaning each of your ongoing learning programs and services should have a business plan, clarifying its role in achieving your objectives. Like strategic plans, business plans are not once-and-done reports to be filed; they are living documents that guide our work.

When I work with clients on crafting business plans for their learning portfolio, we nest the strategy, business plan and implementation plan into one piece of work. When these components are crafted apart from one another, team members setting strategy don't necessarily realize what they are asking program administrators to take on, and staff executing the work are often out of the loop on why they are doing new stuff without new resources. Additionally, when a business plan is updated outside that framework, it loses continuity with the strategic foundation and tactical alignment.

Your business plan should pick up where your education strategy leaves off telling the story of how a program in your portfolio – your annual conference, eLearning, webinars, workshops, regional events, etc. – will contribute to reaching your objectives as both a unique contributor and in collaboration with other programs in your portfolio.

Pause on that thought for a minute.

If we expect our programs to row together toward our goals as a portfolio of learning, we now require alignment. To realize this, we develop a networked and collaborative team culture versus a siloed culture where education programs often compete for resources and power play for favor.

Your business plan should include the following components:

Product-level objectives: How will this program meet overall education strategic objectives as well as what objectives do you specifically have for this product? For example, you may expect eLearning will seek to improve overall revenue and attract young professionals. Objectives: *Our eLearning program will produce courses that support and promote our credential, introduce new voices to our cadre of subject experts, and leverage pricing and promotions to entice nonmembers to convert.* Now you try.

Target audience: Make decisions about primary and secondary audience targets. For large annual conferences, differentiate which experience components target which audience segments. Remember, you cannot design an experience where prospective registrants say, "This is for me!" if you don't have a "me" in mind.

Content priorities: Will this program be in charge of delivering on one of your content priorities? Will it collaborate with other programs to offer a multi-touchpoint experience on your content priorities? What content will be featured? Continuing our eLearning example above, we would primarily target topics related to certification preparation while producing select experiences that would attract a nonmember audience we intend to attract.

Program format: Select program formats that will help you achieve the above.

User experience expectations: Thinking from your target learner profile perspective, what experience points do you desire to deliver? Articulating this assists with identifying the appropriate technology, framing the learning environment, and making five-sense design choices – shifting from what's available and sounds cool to aligning with our experience expectations as a touchstone.

Budget: Simply, include the budget boundaries for this program. When budget line items are significantly different from year-over-year, it's useful to document what that additional sum is intended for or what has been eliminated serving up the savings.

Pricing structure: Detail your price structure and rationale. One of the most repetitive challenges by both participants and volunteer stakeholders is pricing. Give your future self a gift by documenting why the current pricing structure was crafted. What market research supports pricing? What program may be subsidizing this program or what program is this event subsidizing? What past experiences have led to this sound decision? Are you piloting this pricing and looking for specific market input? Keeping your rationale handy and up to date will prepare you for these conversations and ensure important details are not lost.

Marketing goals: Collaborate with your marketing team on crafting goals to prep an intentional campaign and track your success.

Success metrics: Establish the markers that flag all is on track, whether an issue requires intervention, and that you've met your objectives for this program.

This driver asks us whether we have prepared a business plan for each education product/service and whether that business plan is a living document serving as a history of that product's evolution, performance, and goals for what's next. If you just file your business plans, they're busy work. If you leverage them to bridge strategy to action, you're positioned to realize your competitive advantage.

How are we doing?
- ❏ Red (We're not doing this, or, we've started talking about this, but we haven't done anything about it)
- ❏ Yellow (We've taken a few steps toward accomplishing this but have work to do to master this driver area)
- ❏ Green (We're gaining momentum on this, or, we've got a handle on this driver and a plan for what's next)

Action: *What insights have I gleaned, and what next steps are necessary?*

12. Portfolio Evaluation Plan

Outside of the budget report that you look at each month, how do you know whether the programs within your learning portfolio are hitting the mark? Within your business plan you've established objective and metrics. See them through by establishing your portfolio-level evaluation plan.

Our purpose is to measure performance of our learning products and services. There's no reason to wait until the end of a product production cycle to determine success or failure. Our portfolio evaluation plan should be designed to allow us to formatively assess we're on track to hit the success bull's-eye.

Common metrics include
- conversions (are people clicking through emails to your website looking at the registration page and bouncing off? Or are you achieving the conversions you intend?)
- intended audience (are you attracting the audience[s] you've designed a program for? If not, reposition to get traction)
- eLearning utilization (registration, downloads, completion rates)
- referral registrations
- credit claimed, comparing learning programs

- buying cycles (when are learners participating in your different programs over the course of the year; informative for budgeting, launching, marketing)
- number of courses launched
- program-level expenses

The key is to define what a high-functioning learning portfolio looks like and measure your progress toward that target. Your metrics on this level should tell you how well your programs are driving toward your strategic-level objectives, how well individual programs are meeting their own objectives, and operationally, whether the alignment of resources is working as expected. One of the surprises I often see when discussing this driver with clients is the internal versus external insights. We're accustomed to focusing our metrics externally: number of registrants, number of conversions, above-average event evaluations, etc. When we take a look at how programs are administrated internally, organizations often discover surprising inefficiencies to address. Only then can we have a conversation about the root causes.

One example: A client thoughtfully aligned resources with a new online learning initiative, but noted in her program manager's weeklies that production deadlines were not being met despite all the raw materials being available. She pulled the team's timesheets for the past three periods and noted a significant chunk of the day was being spent on handling member calls. At the next team meeting, she facilitated a conversation about what was happening so they could strategize what to do about it. It turns out member services was passing all calls related to online learning to the online education team. They were fielding calls on anything from "how do I log in to my course" to "oops, I purchased a course as a nonmember." With some triage training and a basic LMS administration wiki on SharePoint, the member services team now confidently handles all front-line calls and only escalates technical issues to the online education team, buying back much-needed time in their day to produce awesome online learning programs. Winning all around.

This driver asks us to consider whether

- ⊙ Our portfolio level evaluation plan helps us monitor whether each product is on track or whether tweaks are required to meet our strategic-level and product-level objectives.
- ⊙ We have created a dashboard for these metrics so we can spot trends, intervene as issues arise, and test our budget assumptions (time and money).

How are we doing?

- ❏ Red (We're not doing this, or, we've started talking about this, but we haven't done anything about it)
- ❏ Yellow (We've taken a few steps toward accomplishing this but have work to do to master this driver area)
- ❏ Green (We're gaining momentum on this, or, we've got a handle on this driver and a plan for what's next)

Action: What insights have I gleaned, and what next steps are necessary?

13. Program Policies

One of the natural byproducts of allowing programs to be tucked away in silos is inconsistent policies. Our annual event may have a manual full of policies while webinars are adjudicated one member complaint at a time. The result is inefficiency and variable member experience. Instead, craft a set of policies that are consistent across programs while allowing program specific applications as needed. For example, there should be one policy on copyright ownership and permissions, allowing that eLearning and the annual conference will feature different owned asset examples.

Often when I lead Education Enterprise strategy sessions and we arrive at this driver, knowing looks shoot back and forth across the room when I mention maintaining a program sunset policy. I've lost track of the number of stories about pet programs that staff are pressed to maintain despite its having outlived its life cycle. This persists when we don't have a policy leg to stand on. Buy the ASAE workbook *Focus on What Matters* by Mariah Burton Nelson and make it happen. Your future self thanks you!

One of the other policies I recommend developing is what I affectionately call freshness-dating. When preparing any type of information or learning resource for your constituencies, consider its shelf life. How long should curated content live on your website before you cycle it off? How long should templates live in your member-only resource library until you freshen them up? How long will this recorded session content remain valuable? How long should online programs be offered for sale before they are reviewed for refresh or retirement?

Part of your value proposition is guiding professionals to the resources they need now. If they find stale old stuff and know they can find more recent and relevant resources elsewhere, your brand suffers. I recommend to my clients all digital resources (but especially eLearning) be internally marked for a review cycle. A freshness-dating policy ensures we get eyes on these assets at reasonable intervals as part of our workflow instead of embarrassing back-fills when we realize resources are grossly out of date. In eLearning, this policy should work hand in hand with your course expiry policy to effectively manage your catalog.

This driver asks us to consider whether

⊙ We maintain policies for new program development, program sunset, refund policy, freshness dating, copyright ownership, content licensing, subject expert stipends, noncompliance, crisis communication management, etc.

⊙ Our policies are consistent across products.

How are we doing?

❏ Red (We're not doing this, or, we've started talking about this, but we haven't done anything about it)

❏ Yellow (We've taken a few steps toward accomplishing this but have work to do to master this driver area)

❏ Green (We're gaining momentum on this, or, we've got a handle on this driver and a plan for what's next)

Action: *What insights have I gleaned, and what next steps are necessary?*

14. Learning Environment

When learners enter a session room, the environment sets the table for the type of experience they expect. Each type of learning environment has strengths and weaknesses alongside a range of design choices to produce a particular effect. Upon entering a room, theater seating signals we're about to be entertained and won't likely need to interact with anyone. Rounds or seat groupings suggest there's going to be conversation in the session. Different sitting and standing options tell us we have choice about what level of interaction we desire to engage within the session. Scott Doorley and Scott Witthoft of *Make Space* write about the myriad ways we can use space and furniture to "incite and support specific behaviors." Online, we have an entirely different set of affordances.

The point is this: Impactful learning programs intentionally leverage the learning environment for a particular effect that aligns with our learning experience outcomes.

When viewing our content priorities and target audiences through the learning portfolio lens, we can spot opportunities to leverage different programs staged within different learning environments to our advantage. No more shoe horning sixty-minute recorded lectures into our LMS and calling it eLearning (sixty-minute lectures aren't even good learning in an in-person environment!). Each learning environment can now showcase its strengths, producing meaningful learning experiences.

This driver asks us to consider whether

⊙ Each education program is designed to utilize the strengths of its primary learning environment (live, hybrid, print, online, mobile).

⊙ We design learning environments with our learning objectives and target audience experience in mind.

How are we doing?

❏ Red (We're not doing this, or, we've started talking about this, but we haven't done anything about it)

❏ Yellow (We've taken a few steps toward accomplishing this but have work to do to master this driver area)

❏ Green (We're gaining momentum on this, or, we've got a handle on this driver and a plan for what's next)

Action: What insights have I gleaned, and what next steps are necessary?

15. Content Calendar

Low-hanging fruit alert: Maintain a content calendar.

This driver asks us to consider whether

⊙ We coordinate content deployment to address cycles within the industry.

⊙ We utilize a content calendar so our team can coordinate our content priorities across education and content products in our portfolio.

Consider these three quick-start steps:

First, in your favorite spreadsheet application, draft a calendar showing which learning opportunities are scheduled when within your portfolio and what content they will feature. Upon seeing this data in one place, you may notice your calendar is content heavy or lean at specific times of year. You may determine this is how it should be, but make sure that's an intentional choice. You may notice some topics are hammered heavily while other content priorities aren't getting the same amount of attention. You may notice some boutique content is pulling too many resources or that there's a gap in programming for an audience segment you've targeted to grow. By noticing these incongruities on the portfolio level, you can make different choices.

Most importantly, you may notice there are natural synergies that could be developed among programs that are carrying the conversation around your content priorities through different types of learning experiences. Because these events are already planning to address these topics, it won't take much effort to tie them together and promote each next step in the chain of learning options. By simply viewing our combined content calendar, we introduce powerful opportunities to collaborate among programs.

Second, remember back a few chapters when we walked through crafting an irresistible value proposition – there was a question directly linked to this driver: "Why now?" Your prospect learner opening up your email about an upcoming seminar or online learning course will naturally ask, "Do you want me to participate in this because you're offering this now or because I need it now?" Some topics are pertinent yearlong. Others correspond with cycles within our industry. Maximize the "why now" momentum by coordinating deployment of content in anticipation of needs. Those cycles may also tell you when *not* to offer new programs. Harvest time, tax season, and fall sports physicals are not good times to expect participation in some industries. Consider where industry cycles and content needs intersect. Is everything optimally scheduled?

Third, now that you have your portfolio spreadsheet depicting the coming year, choose one of your content priorities and intentionally weave it throughout your content calendar. Every month use one of your learning programs or communication channels to further the conversation about the topic. With each experience, recommend the next scheduled experience. At the end of the year, curate the touchpoints into a powerful rewind reflection. And promote the next content priority. How does this differ from step one? Intentional coordination. Utilize your content calendar to develop micro-curricula on your content priorities to achieve greater learning outcomes.

What could a first-time-out-of-the-gate micro-curriculum look like?

Scenario: Ethan collaborated with stakeholders and staff to establish his organization's content sandbox and identified five content priorities for coming year. He calls a team meeting with leads from every program in their learning portfolio as well as a couple communication channels; represented are the annual conference, regional event, webinars, eLearning courses, publication, blog, and podcast team leads. He opened the whiteboarding session by acknowledging they wouldn't be able to cover everything there is to know about ethics, but the intent of designing a micro-curriculum for the coming year would be to target gaps in practice that have been identified in the industry where learners need to put the polish on. He turns to draw a simple table on the whiteboard: months of the year on top, all the programs represented down the left. Some events have already staked out dates for the coming year, so they get those up on the board first. Ethan presents their challenge: For the coming year we want to be intentional about advancing the conversation and skill building around ethics by touching our learners with content every month of the coming year. The group brainstorms possibilities and comes up with the following plan.

- Kick it off in January with an **article** in the publication about what's happening in ethics in our field and how learners can get plugged into the conversation this year.
- Develop a series of **blogs** to drop challenging cases; these blog posts are promoted on the LMS portal home page and each include a quiz component on challenging decision points.
- Prepare a series of **podcasts** interviewing people within the industry about an ethical situation – and how it was resolved. Each podcast includes a challenge, obstacles, and resolution learning format. At the end of each, we'll take the opportunity to promote upcoming events – webinar, conference, eLearning. Also promoted on the

LMS portal home page. Delivered on alternate months as ethics blog posts.

- Schedule **webinars** before and after live events to prime and extend learning from those events. We could invite the same or different speakers for those conversations.
- Instead of setting aside courses in the **eLearning** development schedule addressing ethics this year, each course will include an ethics segment related to the topic. Those segments could be curated later into a full-length course if we choose.
- Midyear we'll schedule an **article** to advance the topic in our publication and do a *review/preview* of our programming. And we conclude the year with an article retracing our steps, testimonials, and links to what's still available because the FOMO is growing.
- Anyone who enrolls in a program is notified of future learning opportunities in this focus area and when content drops. We'll utilize registration lists to invite learners to continue participating in the unfolding content conversation.

Notice the advantages of this approach. We have not purchased any new technology or launched a new program, we have simply, and deliberately, coordinated a content priority through existing opportunities in our portfolio to achieve a greater objective than a once-and-done session could ever hope for. Each of these touchpoints is an opportunity to tee up the next. All this goes without saying. We are already serving up content through each of these channels – *why not* coordinate our portfolio around our priorities to elevate the experience, punch up the impact, and share the content development load across programs?

There is no catch here. All this requires is coordination. You can do this!

How are we doing?
- ❏ Red (We're not doing this, or, we've started talking about this, but we haven't done anything about it)
- ❏ Yellow (We've taken a few steps toward accomplishing this but have work to do to master this driver area)
- ❏ Green (We're gaining momentum on this, or, we've got a handle on this driver and a plan for what's next)

Action: What insights have I gleaned, and what next steps are necessary?

16. Learning Pathways

If you enjoyed the last driver, learning pathways are next-level awesome.

Before the big reveal, a hard truth: Learning is *not* an event.

Now in stereo: Learning is not an event. Learning is a process.

So despite the fact it is convenient for us to offer "learning events," not much learning happens unless we are tapping into the learning process. Learning science tells us what happens before and after a learning episode (and we're assuming the episode is designed to be learning, not just deliver information) is more important than the session itself. You can read more about this in *The Six Disciplines of Breakthrough Learning* by Roy Pollock et al. All this to say, if informing is your goal, a session works great. If learning is your goal – increasing knowledge base, deepening understanding, improving critical thinking, enhancing skill, developing mastery – we have to think beyond the session.

Coordinating content within our content calendar is a great way to begin building connective tissue between programs allowing us to meaningfully advance a conversation around a topic instead of serving up disparate pieces. Learning pathways takes this idea to the next level by developing stepping-stones toward mastery.

Think about a skill you've developed – something you excel at. It could be rebuilding engines or auditing complex organizations or designing successful business models. How did you come to master this skill? Was it from attending sessions at events that were topically related but presented by different speakers with their individual take that didn't directly connect with previous event presentations? Not likely. Because that's not how brains develop mastery.

There's a long-version and short-version explanation of the science of mastery. Here's the short version. To facilitate learning, we must address the entire learning cycle (more on that in driver 19) and coordinate learning experiences that serve as a pathway to mastery. The end game is developing curriculum around critical knowledge and skills (you define what's critical for your organization and your industry). A first step to piloting this is coordinating event-based learning pathways.

Event-based learning pathways allow us to start where we are with our current learning portfolio and develop a skill-based learning experience. Fan out your learning program and content channels like an excellent hand at the beginning of a Hearts game. Lay out your before, during, and after (BDA) game plan: What will happen before the learning event, during, and after the event to support your learning objectives?

Before: Offer at least one priming opportunity to set expectations, initiate thinking in the direction of the learning objectives, and/or consume a piece of content that will be applied during content delivery.

During: Facilitate a learning experience aligned with how brains acquire new knowledge and skill. Offer optional discovery material so participants know where to go in your learning portfolio or curated resources to dig deeper or take a next step.

After: Offer performance support. By far the biggest part of the learning process is transferring ideas to practice, applying them, overcoming obstacles, refining our approach, and making the knowledge our own.

Let's visualize this with an example.

Scenario: Tiana's association offers a two-day leadership event each year. Even though industry pros say leadership development is critical, registration in this event is disappointing. She decides to assemble the team to imagine how they could elevate the quality and impact of this experience by building a learning pathway around it. Tiana draws a rectangle on her screen representing the event. She introduces the BDA approach and kicks off the brainstorm with the question: *How can we ensure learners are primed and ready for this new workshop experience?* Next, they talk about how they'll need to reformat the event into a workshop, allowing space for peer interaction, exercises, and action planning. Tiana asks the team, *what resources could we develop or already exist that we could offer for learners to dig deeper on their own?* Finally, Tiana challenges the team to think about the real impact they want to see from this workshop that members are clamoring for. She asks the team, *how can we support participants applying what they learned when they get back to the office?*

Here's the pilot plan:

In collaboration with the education committee, develop learning outcomes and select four experts to each design a half-day workshop experience aligning with those outcomes.

Before the event, interview the experts for an article published before the workshop offering a few key concepts that workshop attendees will really get to explore. The article is expected to drive additional registration and prepare learner expectations, priming them for the event. We'll include a link in the "before you arrive" registrant email.

Before the event, interview the experts individually for a podcast series that will be delivered in the months after the workshop, recapping nuggets from workshop core concepts. Podcasts recap key content for participants, encouraging application. They can also be used to promote next year's workshop.

Before the event, request each expert contribute a blog post on one key point from their presentation published during the event with links to additional online info to explore. Our publication team will also curate links of recommended materials. This supports discovery learning.

For the event, each expert will contribute a resource or tool (not their slide deck) for participants that can be added to your member-only online resource library. Tools could be a job aid, checklist, template, process, etc. (more on this in driver 23).

After the event, host a follow-up webinar discussion to extend the conversation about applying the strategies addressed in the workshop in day-to-day practice. Speakers will not prepare new content but will facilitate a dialogue about obstacles and overcoming them.

A selection of these components will be featured in an eNews rewind article with links to access each. Prominently featured will be participant recommendations for this impactful experience and a save-the-date for next year.

The result: This is no longer a one-off event. We have effectively maximized the content, maximized the collaboration with our experts, extended the learning from curiosity to application, and extended the reach of the content to a broader audience without cannibalizing our event. And all that is required is planning and coordination.

OK, so why is this important?

By paying attention to designing readiness material and follow-up material when learners are back in their day-to-day context, studies show we can significantly increase the effectiveness of learning. This is where we become meaningful and memorable. This is where employers see the difference our continuing education makes. This is when both learner and employer recognize the results of participating in our programs.

This is a significant differentiator – and part of what will give you the competitive advantage.

Now you try. Pick a skill and an event. Design a before, during, and after learning pathway to prepare participants to learn, facilitate learning at the event, and support application (we call this transfer) after the event where real learning takes place.

This driver asks us to consider whether

⊙ Our content priorities guide coordinated learning pathway development.

⊙ We employ learning pathways – coordinating multiple touchpoints across education products to extend learning into the context of application for greater outcomes.

⊙ We employ learning pathways to deepen our relationship with members and member prospects as an indispensable in-time resource.

How are we doing?

❑ Red (We're not doing this, or, we've started talking about this, but we haven't done anything about it)

❑ Yellow (We've taken a few steps toward accomplishing this but have work to do to master this driver area)

❑ Green (We're gaining momentum on this, or, we've got a handle on this driver and a plan for what's next)

Action: What insights have I gleaned, and what next steps are necessary?

17. Education Technology Management

EdTech is a new frontier for many of us, offering rich new possibilities for engaging learners and elevating the online learning experience. For an association, technologies supporting education range from online registration and automatic response systems (ARS) to your learning management system and learner community hub. You could also toss into that mix your apps, online catalog storefront, and rapid development software – anything that integrates with and supports the learning experience.

Unfortunately, EdTech is not like a new Amana refrigerator that you plug in and let run for a decade. It requires leadership. It requires strategy and management. It requires you to pay attention to the experience because the technology just does what you tell it to do.

This driver asks us to be mindful of education technology management. For example, when we're strategizing our online learning experience, we're noting our system requirements as well as our feature wish list so we can proactively align needs with system capabilities. We're also mindful of the experience we're providing from click to click by walking through the workflows as if following members and nonmembers through each process. (Learn more about the "staple" technique here: https://hbr.org/2004/07/staple-yourself-to-an-order.)

If no one has their eye on this ball, it's going to get away from you.

This driver asks us to consider whether

- ⊙ We have defined our digital learning system requirements and communicate our present and future needs to our LMS solution partner to ensure we are maximizing its capabilities.
- ⊙ Our EdTech systems are intuitive to navigate and mindful how many clicks are required to complete a transaction.
- ⊙ We routinely "staple ourselves to a learner" to better understand our members' experiences (across member types) as a form of QA testing and feedback for improvement.

How are we doing?
- ❏ Red (We're not doing this, or, we've started talking about this, but we haven't done anything about it)
- ❏ Yellow (We've taken a few steps toward accomplishing this but have work to do to master this driver area)
- ❏ Green (We're gaining momentum on this, or, we've got a handle on this driver and a plan for what's next)

Action: What insights have I gleaned, and what next steps are necessary?

18. Customer Service

Regardless whether you have an in-house member service team dedicated to answering calls or each staff person is responsible to pick up the mainline when it rings, you need a customer service plan for your learning portfolio. Association leadership rarely realizes the significant amount of staff time devoted to finding answers to member questions that could be mitigated with a little plan prep.

Your customer service plan encompasses all the ways you efficiently get accurate information to those who are asking. You may start by assessing the content on your website and whether members can find the answers they need. Prepare internal FAQs so those answering the phones have quick access to up-to-date information, new program features, and upcoming program launches. Track frequent issues so you can discuss how to mitigate them. Create a process for escalating issues to the appropriate person. Have a plan for handling crisis situations – anything from bed bugs at your conference hotel to your webinar vendor's platform crashing just before your virtual event goes live (both real instances!).

This driver asks us to consider whether

⊙ We maintain a customer service plan for all education products, ensuring members know how to access the support they need for an optimal experience.

⊙ We employ a triage process to address issues with education programs, partnering with member services on frequently asked questions and utilizing program administrators for technical questions.

⊙ We have emergency protocol in place for our events – live or digital disruptions.

How are we doing?

❏ Red (We're not doing this, or, we've started talking about this, but we haven't done anything about it)

❏ Yellow (We've taken a few steps toward accomplishing this but have work to do to master this driver area)

❏ Green (We're gaining momentum on this, or, we've got a handle on this driver and a plan for what's next)

Action: What insights have I gleaned, and what next steps are necessary?

Start Where You Are

You have everything you need to begin strategically leveraging your learning portfolio. Today, without launching a new program, subscribing to new technology, or hiring a new team member, you can shed your event-based blinders for a portfolio point of view. Not only will you be able to find efficiencies that will decrease your expenses, but you will also be able to develop program synergies that will significantly improve your value. Coincidentally, both translate into bigger bang for your budget.

That's the good news.

The other good news is this: If you want the competitive advantage edge, these drivers are key. The old model of isolated one-off events is not sustainable in a world demanding 24/7 access to learning that results in transformation. Lay out your portfolio of options to discover ripe opportunities to produce powerful experiences with touchpoints over time that usher learners through pathways of mastery – the result they want within your learning curriculum – instead of the event registration revolving door. Uncover new efficiencies by simply becoming more intentional and minding what program administration requires behind the scenes.

Is change hard? It can be, but it doesn't have to be. It's exactly what we make of it. You have all the ingredients for sustainable continuing education programs. Put them to work.

REFLECTION

- ⊙ Review your ratings for each driver. Which sounds like it would produce the greatest gains to pursue?
- ⊙ Which event in your portfolio would be a great candidate for a learning pathway pilot?
- ⊙ What opportunities for alignment between your strategic objectives and taking on a portfolio point of view could produce some quick wins for you?

Chapter 6:

Don't Feed the Silos

"I can sum up all our problems in a few words:
silos and butt-covering."

JOHN G. MILLER, QBQ: THE QUESTION BEHIND THE QUESTION

When I consult with organizations that hire me after taking a few running starts at a strategic initiative, I do a couple key things. First, I look at what's been done. In many cases, the flaw is not the work. Next, I gather the team and ask them why they think this has happened and why they think this time with me will be different.

Has this happened at your organization? You've tried some things, but they didn't stick? You assembled a task force and poured a ton of staff hours into an event, a curriculum, a competency model, a new process, but it just didn't work its way into the muscle? Perhaps after a pilot or two it fell away and old defaults reengaged.

We know we need to do something different.

I confirm with some humor to my clients that they did make an amazing choice selecting me, that I'm thrilled to partner with them, and that our work together will be well worth it. But the truth is, it's not just me that's the "something different."

Sustainability is in the room.

The solution to this repeating pattern is not a thing. It's not the strategy, curriculum, course, learning design template, or technology. Those are tools we need, and it's easy to assign that value marker to the "thing" because that work product feels tangible. So that must be the "something different." I reveal to my clients frankly that in our work together you will get things. Lots of high-quality, top-shelf things. But those things alone are not the solution to the sustainability issue.

The solution, the "something different," is a way of thinking and operationalizing this work.

Sustainability is us. It's in this room. It's you. Your talent, priority alignment, accountability, and processes.

Silos are a choice. Good work losing to default habits and preferences is a choice. Sustainability of our strategic objective implementation is a matter of thinking differently and collaborating differently – operationalizing our work from a portfolio perspective.

That's the something different.

And that's what our Portfolio Management Drivers ask us to consider.

By managing our programs as a portfolio of learning, we significantly increase opportunities for discovering program management efficiencies (which save us time and money). Even greater, we are now positioned to collaboratively produce learning pathways that deliver the results members desire.

But what happens if you decide not to implement a portfolio perspective?

- ⊙ **Persistent silos.** It's important to have the right talent around your education programs, but teams don't need to be siloed. Organizations that allow programs to be sequestered to siloed teams can expect those silos will have their own agenda and act in the silo's best interest. Silos negatively impact organization culture and the member experience.
- ⊙ **Program competition.** Organizations that don't manage their learning programs as a portfolio experience competitiveness between programs instead of cooperativeness. Silos encourage this. It manifests in mini-kingdoms where information is less likely to be shared and turf wars, resource grabs, and a lack of trust reign. All of this ultimately results in poor decision-making.
- ⊙ **Piece-meal programs.** Our status quo pile of rocks will persist. We'll offer piecemeal programs on topics but not bother with full learning cycles or offering pathways to mastery. Without taking the effort to build a content calendar and coordinate our learning resources, we offer members some but not all pieces to

a very complex knowledge puzzle. This environment is not friendly to producing results-based learning.

- ⊙ **Hidden performance issues.** When we're only measuring how our programs are developing in comparison with how we've "done it before," a lot of important data sits in your blind spot. Instead, our Portfolio Management Drivers are asking us to measure whether programs are on target with our overall strategic objectives in addition to program-level goals. We are also measuring the administration of programs so we can spot performance issues and introduce efficiencies that make room for expanded capacity. We can also spot opportunities to reduce re-work. Why allow needless inefficiencies to persist?

- ⊙ **Inconsistent Policies.** Policies are our friend. They prepare us for eventualities so we can engage consistent business practices and don't have to reinvent our response on the fly – opening the door to critical errors. This is such an easy fix. Why risk poor decision-making under pressure when you can anticipate the best course of action and have exception-based conversations if the need arises. Consistency improves the member experience and saves untold hours of staff time.

- ⊙ **Sustainability fails.** Even if you have developed an education strategy, if you do not operationalize it throughout your portfolio of learning, it will be terribly difficult to sustain. Visionary plans for innovation often become mired in the mini-kingdom ways of doing things. And all that great work quietly disappears without accountability to collaborative teaming within your portfolio, and sometimes across organizational divisions.

Red Light, Green Light

I don't typically see a lot of green lights in the Portfolio Management Drivers in my consulting. Thinking about education programs as a learning portfolio is often a new concept. I honor your green lights; build on them as you expand to the other drivers to increase your learning delivery effectiveness and impact.

If you scored your organization yellow on a majority of the Portfolio Management Drivers, I suspect you also noted a lot of low-hanging fruit you can address for some quick wins. Often many of the components of a business plan are scattered among files and can easily be assembled so objectives and metrics can be clarified. Often there are some policies in place, and it's an easy fix to bring standardization across programs. Typically, we have customer service protocols in place but can take intentional steps to improve the experience. I encourage you to give the content calendar driver a try. You'll naturally discover synergies among programs you can proactively connect. Pilot a learning pathway, measuring the dramatically different results in learning outcomes. And take time to develop your portfolio evaluation plan. Consider both how programs are performing according to your expectations for learners and how they are performing operationally.

If you scored in the red zone for the Portfolio Management Drivers, begin your efforts by thinking about the role each program in your portfolio will play to advance your strategic objectives (part of business planning). Then craft your portfolio evaluation plan. These two steps will advance your efforts toward developing a dashboard that will guide strategy through implementation, creating new expectations for how teams will coordinate efforts.

Your Competitive Advantage

A portfolio perspective introduces significant opportunity for program management efficiencies and a unified member experience with your brand. It's an operational structure that is compatible with maximizing current program resources to deliver learning experiences that result in mastery. It's calling on us to embrace our education strategy as a portfolio team – sustaining innovation as we reach for greater impact within the industries we represent.

With our strategy and portfolio management lenses in place, let's explore the third set of drivers challenging us to design learning experiences that make a measurable impact.

Chapter 7:
Learning Design

*"We need to bring learning to people
instead of people to learning."*
ELLIOTT MASIE

U.S. Bank Stadium

One of the greatest live-action spectacles I've witnessed is the construction of U.S. Bank Stadium, the Minnesota Vikings' new home.

I worked in downtown Minneapolis just a few blocks away from the construction site. There was a constant flow of people (like me!) stopping by year-round to witness this enormous new landmark take shape. What started as a crater where the "Metro Muffin" used to be was a massive project with twice the footprint. The U.S. Bank Stadium has six levels spanning 1.75 million square feet, five giant hydraulic pivoting glass doors, several massive video boards (one is 8,160 square feet), works from forty local artists, and 979 restrooms (thank you!) and is probably the only stadium with heated snow gutters (because #Minnesnowta). It took about three years to complete and cost a touch over $1 billion. Just in time to host Super Bowl LII.

So many things needed to happen before the public was invited inside the fully loaded stadium. Before tricking out the décor or selling tickets, we had to scaffold the structure and fill it in piece by piece.

This is very similar to the learning brain – physically and metaphorically. We start with a foundation and a plan. We scaffold the structure of knowledge we intend to impart and fill it in piece by piece until it's complete. We can't start with the roof. We can't start with the concession menus. We start with learner's foundation and build a new knowledge structure from their leaving-off point. Think about the knowledge domain you represent as a high-rise; your learner may have four well-developed floors and is framing in the fifth. How do you design your learning opportunities to meet them where they are? First filling in the foundation, then the structure, then the nuance of the subject.

This is required to build new memories leading to lasting learning. And it doesn't happen by accident, it happens by design: Instructional Design.

Often in conference breakout sessions, I ask attendees whether their association either has instructional designers on staff or at least contracts with one to design their learning programs. More often than not, I can count the yes's on one hand (typically two fingers). What this means is we're leaving our education programs to chance, throwing spaghetti against a wall and hoping a few strands will stick. We're expecting to be able to build a stadium that fans will flock to without a coordinated plan that will achieve our goals.

Instead of trying to win the education program lottery hoping for quality learning to happen by sheer luck, we can ensure a learning win by design.

What happens when we apply instructional design to our learning opportunities? The three Ms: learning becomes *meaningful, memorable,* and *measurable.*

Meaningful. Learners enroll in our courses, register for our conferences, and attend our programs because they are looking for meaningful content. Content that is relevant. That will solve a problem. That will increase skill. Something they can use right now. And once they are sitting in our classrooms, meaning is vital to achieving learner engagement. Learners have so many options to choose from for their lifelong learning. Make the most of their goodwill enrolling in your programs by designing a meaningful learning experience. Employ the full learning cycle to ensure sessions are designed from the moment of grabbing attention to application. Design programs to connect to learner's prior knowledge and skill base (remember their skyscraper levels!), connecting the dots to personal relevance.

Memorable. Too often we provide learners information, not learning experiences. When we leave learning design to chance, more often than not we present ideas but don't structure the opportunity to support actual learning. To ensure learning happens, sessions must be designed to support memory development and application. Courses that do not incorporate opportunities for reflection, articulation, collaboration, and application shouldn't really be called education. We can easily stand apart among the spectrum of continuing education options by incorporating remembering strategies into our course design – designing content to be transferred to real-world practice. If the content you offer is not only meaningful to learners but also improves lives when applied in practice, you can expect learner loyalty and your net promoter value to skyrocket.

Measurable. When learning opportunities are designed to meet measurable objectives, you can finally evaluate the quality and impact of your programs. Measure that learning has happened. Measure the workplace impact of your training (and use that to strengthen the value proposition of your programs). Measure the outcomes of participating in your certification programs. Measure the ROI of your education programs now that you've determined what success looks like and implemented it in your course design. Want to substantiate the value of your programs, the need for growth in your budget, or convince your board to support a new program? Measure what matters. Stop measuring "likes" and start measuring impact. You can do this when programs are intentionally designed with your measures for success in mind.

Learning design is a key missing ingredient in so many programs that really want to be education. And it's required to establish your competitive advantage.

Learning Design Drivers

A commitment to learning design differentiates your programs from the competition, resulting in increased registration, net promoter ratings, revenue, and most of all, impact. Open your journal one last time and rate your organization on the following drivers.

19. Instructional Design

If you want to advance your competitive advantage, this driver is not just a nice-to-have. It's a requirement.

Ultimately, the success of program execution comes down to learning design. You can have an amazing strategy and set up inspired collaborations within your portfolio. But if you're just turning on the content firehose, you may as well just save the water. And don't call it education.

Learning is change. Learning programs are designed to facilitate transformation.

Quick story: Earlier in my career I was a communications instructor at a liberal arts college in St. Paul, Minnesota. I remember so clearly walking into that classroom the first day fresh out of graduate school with my textbook and all sorts of enthusiasm. I felt confident, having been a TA for several courses and, well, I even took a pedagogy class so how hard could this be?

I could immediately see before my eyes when my methods succeeded or epically failed. Just the fact that I was enthusiastic about the subject had little to no bearing on whether my students cared or engaged. I realized quickly I had a lot to learn. Since I really wanted to succeed more than fail, I became deeply inspired to study everything I could get my hands on regarding adult learning design and the learning sciences – so I could understand how and why brains learn and bring those principles forward in my work.

As a result, my communications studies classroom became my laboratory. I dug deeper into course outcomes and worked to ensure our classroom sessions were not just textbook regurgitations but a safe place to observe concepts in action and experiment with new skills. Each speech project built on the next one as I evolved my course curriculum – no more random assignments and busy work. My students became more invested because they could see a direct correlation between each activity and our end result goals (our learning objectives).

They could envision the learning journey.

Now did all these epiphanies occur overnight or even within the span of one semester? Nope! I learned from both my successes and failures. The good news is that my research paid off. That course was run internationally, both on campus and through distance learning. And my continued research has resulted in the distillation of the 4A Learning Cycle Model that we now use at InspirEd for our clients.

To make training effective, we need to approach our education not as info dumping grounds but as meaningful learning experiences. We must approach our training from a learner-centric posture, understanding how the brain learns and what brains expect when it's time to acquire new knowledge, skills, and competencies.

We chat about this concept briefly earlier when introducing the Learning Pathway driver. Learning is not an event, it's a process. So, depending on the scope of your learning objectives, you may or may not be able to fit an entire learning cycle in one session. The value is not content. *The value is transformation.* It's time to rethink how we can deliver that.

Instructional design is not a format, a software, a copy/paste framework, or even ADDIE (Hint: It's a "D" in ADDIE). It is an expertise and practice informed by learning science that results in measurable change. It capitalizes on predictable brain processes for acquiring new knowledge or skill, so we can design intentional experiences that ultimately trigger transformation in the learner. By employing the best practices of instructional design, we have the power to make intentional choices for facilitating the journey from where a learner presently is to where we'd like to safely deliver them in their journey to mastery.

Unfortunately, it is also a missing ingredient in most PowerPoint presentations crafted for "learning" sessions by well-meaning industry experts. They need our instructional design guidance and partnership.

Embracing learning design is necessary to differentiate our programs. And the measurable outcomes can be leveraged to promote your competitive advantage.

This driver asks us to evaluate whether

⊙ Each learning event utilizes instructional design best practices for the adult learner.

- ⊙ Our programs are designed as meaningful (relevant to learner) and memorable (employing remembering strategies) experiences versus information sessions.
- ⊙ We seek to offer full learning-cycle education (attend, analyze, associate, apply), whether that be within one event or facilitated over a series of touchpoints.

How are we doing?
- ❏ Red (We're not doing this, or, we've started talking about this, but we haven't done anything about it)
- ❏ Yellow (We've taken a few steps toward accomplishing this but have work to do to master this driver area)
- ❏ Green (We're gaining momentum on this, or, we've got a handle on this driver and a plan for what's next)

Action: *What insights have I gleaned, and what next steps are necessary?*

20. Competency Development

Competencies are the new currency in workforce development.

Once upon a time, we would get some education (could be vocational, apprenticeship, or higher ed) and then get a job. We would work for that employer for many, many years and likely not even dream about hopping over to another industry. That's just how it was.

It's dramatically different now. Even in industries where professionals invest in extended training to become lawyers, doctors and CPAs, we *still* see career switch departures. We're not bound to stay in one lane anymore. No matter the years in training to get in the lane.

As a result, we're seeing a surge in certificate programs and certifications to prove worth to prospect employers as we navigate career lattices. Mozilla Backpack entered the scene in 2012 with the vision of open badges referencing verifiable credentials and achievements collected in a portable and publicly presentable format. Beginning in 2017, Credential Engine went live with its registry, matching credentialing programs with prospect credential earners as well as employers comparing credential apples and oranges.

In response to this significant movement underway, many organizations have placed "badges" and "backpacks" on committee agendas and featured conference sessions on "developing badges" while missing the point entirely. The point is not the badge or the portfolio that holds them. The value is *competency*, an externally validated capability to *do* or *be* something. Given the time and expense of a new formal degree is not in the cards for most considering a career move, professionals are seeking reputable sources for upskilling, retooling, and verifying portable skills and competencies.

Which brings us back to this driver. If our programs are primarily information based, we're not meeting this need in our industry.

If our programs are only designed to develop knowledge and understanding, we're not meeting this need in our industry.

If our programs are offering knowledge and some skill-based experiences but not offering pathways toward mastery, we're not meeting this need in our industry.

I'm not the only one talking about the importance of competency-based learning. Your competitors will figure this out if they haven't already. If your organization is not deliberately designing curriculum intending to develop competencies, this needs to be agenda item No. 1.

Does every program need to be competency based and part of an integrated curriculum? No, it doesn't. But in the current continuing education market, skipping this driver is a big risk if you desire to stay competitive.

This driver asks us to consider whether
- ⊙ [Basic] We maintain a list of core competencies based on stakeholder consensus that informs curriculum development for our industry.
- ⊙ [Advanced] We maintain a validated competency model that informs curriculum development for our industry.
- ⊙ We offer programs aligned with our competency model, offering pathways to skill development and mastery.

How are we doing?
- ❏ Red (We're not doing this, or, we've started talking about this, but we haven't done anything about it)
- ❏ Yellow (We've taken a few steps toward accomplishing this but have work to do to master this driver area)

❏ Green (We're gaining momentum on this, or, we've got a handle on this driver and a plan for what's next)

Action: *What insights have I gleaned, and what next steps are necessary?*

21. Learning Evaluation

How do you use your course evaluations? Do they return actionable insights on how to improve learning outcomes? Do your course evaluations actually evaluate learning?

There are several common errors in the majority of course evaluations.

⊙ Asking about agreement and satisfaction
⊙ Believing Likert scale "pen scores" carry statistical validity
⊙ Asking "what *topics* would you like to see in future programs"

Now that we're embracing learning design in our programs, our evaluations should measure learning. We have a history of allowing speakers to run our education programs for us, so naturally we have developed evaluation instruments that measure whether people like them or not so we can gauge whether or not to invite them again. Also, whether we, incidentally, need to make any logistical tweaks next time.

Instead, measure whether learning happened.

Because if a speaker has an amazing "like" rating and participants don't apply or do anything differently after the session, *that's a fail.*

Whiteboard this checklist against your current evaluation form:

- ⊙ We measure the learning objectives were met – whether they intended to impact understanding or skill development
- ⊙ Any questions using scales define explicitly what each point on the scale means to remove ambiguity and bias. Reference Will Thalheimer's book Performance-Focused Smile Sheets[10] for examples.
- ⊙ Measure confidence and commitment levels in applying new knowledge/skills
- ⊙ If you're measuring competencies, use mixed methods to measure whether behavior has changed. Reference Kirkpatrick's Four Levels of Training Evaluation[11] for examples.
- ⊙ Ask a net promoter score question to understand what participants really think about the value of your program.

Additionally, instead of asking for "topics," ask what obstacles learners are facing in practice, what problems they desire to solve, or what resources they need to improve their knowledge and skill. By asking these questions, instead of getting the one-word answer "leadership" as an important topic, you will receive valuable insights on barriers within the learner's current context, the specific tools or support that would matter to their practice, and greater specificity – maybe the leadership issue is really managing a passive aggressive employee or cultivating influence within the organization. You can do a lot more with all that information than the one-word answer "leadership."

Execution Tip: You may have noticed three Scorecard drivers address evaluation. I recommend rolling your three-level evaluation plan into your dashboard so you can see the congruities, vision to execution successes, and realign any aspects that are wavering from your intended targets.

This driver asks us to evaluate whether

- ⊙ Each learning event has been designed to measure that learning objectives have been achieved – which means objectives are measurable and we measure them.

- ⊙ We measure Kirkpatrick Levels 1 and 2 at minimum and seek opportunities to extend our evaluation to Levels 3 and 4 to demonstrate the value of our programs to our multiple constituencies. We are explicit about what we are measuring and tie these results to the goals we have for the program – so we can make data-based decisions.

How are we doing?

- ❑ Red (We're not doing this, or, we've started talking about this, but we haven't done anything about it)

❏ Yellow (We've taken a few steps toward accomplishing this but have work to do to master this driver area)
❏ Green (We're gaining momentum on this, or, we've got a handle on this driver and a plan for what's next)

Action: What insights have I gleaned, and what next steps are necessary?

22. Design Process

This driver is a love letter to learning pros developing online learning experiences. Associations typically have detailed processes for live events and conferences – enough to fill an Access database and overwhelm even the most motivated list maker. We know weeks out from an event what should have been accomplished and what's next to make sure we're on pace for a successful event. We also allot this courtesy to publications, accepting that they operate on a framework of rolling deadline cogs and wheels that result in our magazine or journal. Too often, our webinars, eLearning, and pilot learning programs are left without this same support.

This driver asks us to acknowledge that learning programs we produce do have a design process. The process will be different for events than enduring online learning (which requires maintenance cycles). Regardless, there are a standard set of affordances for all project-based work. And we should articulate those processes so we allow adequate and sustainable production timelines.

This driver asks us to evaluate whether

⊙ We embrace a program design process for learning events that includes: analyzing need, stakeholder kick off, design, production, QA testing, evaluation, documenting, results/insights, and recommendations for the next iteration.

⊙ Our design timelines are adequate and sustainable.

How are we doing?

❏ Red (We're not doing this, or, we've started talking about this, but we haven't done anything about it)

❏ Yellow (We've taken a few steps toward accomplishing this but have work to do to master this driver area)

❏ Green (We're gaining momentum on this, or, we've got a handle on this driver and a plan for what's next)

Action: What insights have I gleaned, and what next steps are necessary?

23. Transformational Learning Tools

Why do learners ask for program PowerPoint decks? Is it because they intend to kick back in the easy chair and flip through hundreds of slides recalling our good times together? Not likely. I witness three reasons:

⊙ Participants believe that deck is part of the value – they are not getting full *value* for the program through the *experience*. (Also, you've conditioned them in this belief and allowed speakers to submit slideument eBooks versus presentation aids.)

⊙ The sessions are a content fire hose, so participants figure by collecting the PowerPoint decks, they'll be able to someday find time to digest what they missed.

⊙ The speaker offered some best practice nuggets, a process diagram, a checklist or additional references, so participants think they'll find time to distill these tools from the deck so they can do something with the content afterward.

All these reasons mean we have not designed transformational learning that supports transfer and application. And the hard truth is, providing the slide deck will not help learners achieve their learning goals.

Instead, offer transformational learning tools.

When asking speakers to submit their session materials, ask them to distill the tool(s) from their presentation: the best practice nuggets, process diagram, checklist, template, or additional references. This is the material learners really want so they can do something about this content. These are the items they are clamoring for in your digital resource library. These are the high-value enduring bits branded to your organization that end up tucked in planners and pinned up in cubicles.

Instead of slide decks, offer tools and resources for application and deeper discovery that support the full learning cycle.

This driver asks us to evaluate whether

- ⊙ We prioritize job aids, checklists, processes specs, self-assessments, coaching, and other application tools over offering PowerPoint presentations as learning and transfer support.
- ⊙ We intentionally partner informational and learning opportunities understanding they are different experiences with different outcomes.

How are we doing?
- ❏ Red (We're not doing this, or, we've started talking about this, but we haven't done anything about it)
- ❏ Yellow (We've taken a few steps toward accomplishing this but have work to do to master this driver area)
- ❏ Green (We're gaining momentum on this, or, we've got a handle on this driver and a plan for what's next)

Action: *What insights have I gleaned, and what next steps are necessary?*

24. Visual Design

Visual design is vital to a learning experience, loaded with the potential to either crystallize or cripple understanding.

No pressure.

It's true, though. Studies show poor visual design depresses learning. Effective visual design, however, grabs attention, makes connections, fosters idea associations, and paves the way for applying new ideas in practice. Visuals help us think and process information.

So, who is designing visuals for your courses, both in person and online?

This driver asks us to acknowledge that the visuals used in a learning session are consequential. There are best practices for designing visuals for learning so you can better collaborate with your subject matter experts to craft visuals that support learning outcomes. I offer a free eBook, *Visual Design Essentials*, calling out the chief offenders in poorly designed visuals, checklists for evaluating designs, resources you'll want to follow up on, and a bonus section on screen design considerations. Feel free to grab a copy, no strings attached: http://tracy-king.com/resources/

This driver asks us to evaluate whether
- ⊙ We utilize best practices in visual design and media production for our learning events.
- ⊙ We offer design support to SMEs developing slide presentations or other learning resources.

How are we doing?
- ❏ Red (We're not doing this, or, we've started talking about this, but we haven't done anything about it)
- ❏ Yellow (We've taken a few steps toward accomplishing this but have work to do to master this driver area)
- ❏ Green (We're gaining momentum on this, or, we've got a handle on this driver and a plan for what's next)

Action: What insights have I gleaned, and what next steps are necessary?

25. SME Development

By now you've likely asked yourself, *How am I going to get my SMEs to do all of this?* Or maybe, *This is impossible! Except that transformational tools thing, I think we can do that.*

Both are very common responses and why we save this juicy driver for last. Historically, our event success has hinged on what speakers (often volunteers) contribute. We have become accustomed to taking what they offer with minimal feedback, accountability, or support. We're "getting content out there," but it is not the experience that will generate a competitive advantage.

If we are committed to differentiating our programs, producing impactful learning experiences, and advancing the professionalism of our industry, we must commit to partnering with our SMEs. This should take the form of learning design support from staff, acquiring quality training resources, and creating a feedback loop. Essentially, serving as a SME should be a learning opportunity for your presenters. This is your organization's investment in driving toward your experience outcomes while elevating the pool of presenters to greater effectiveness. Win-win-win.

This driver asks us to evaluate whether
- We work train and work with our SMEs to execute learning events demonstrating the best practices of learning design we are committed to delivering on.
- We offer feedback and accountability to our speakers and online learning SMEs.

How are we doing?
- ❏ Red (We're not doing this, or, we've started talking about this, but we haven't done anything about it)
- ❏ Yellow (We've taken a few steps toward accomplishing this but have work to do to master this driver area)
- ❏ Green (We're gaining momentum on this, or, we've got a handle on this driver and a plan for what's next)

Action: What insights have I gleaned, and what next steps are necessary?

Linchpin

If you're satisfied with being a reputable source of information and comfortable setting the content buffet while foregoing responsibility for the results – I congratulate you for getting this far into the book, but it's not for you. Bless you in your efforts to compete with Google and Amazon.

If you're concerned about cultivating a qualified pipeline for your industry, helping professionals upskill and retool to meet changing demands, amplifying the professionalism of your industry, defining the competencies that will distinguish high performers, and leading the way to a successful and satisfying career though mastery – you now have a blueprint to build that dream.

Learning design is the linchpin for making an impact that matters.

REFLECTION

- ⊙ Review your ratings for each driver. Which are of greatest priority?
- ⊙ If the Instructional Design driver is rated red or yellow, what next step(s) will you commit to embracing transformational learning design for your programs?
- ⊙ What opportunities for introducing learning design in your portfolio do you notice that could produce some quick wins for your association?

Chapter 8:
Paper Airplane Potential

"Change is the end result of all true learning."
LEO BUSCAGLIA

It bears repeating: If people leave a session or course and do nothing, we have failed.

Allow that to sink in.

Even if the speaker receives top scores and attendees high five and say "fun event," if they leave and do nothing, try nothing, change nothing, learning did not happen.

Are you OK with that?

I see a lot of gatherings called education sessions or courses where information is shared. There may even be a case presented. But if the content isn't transferable, it's still like a presenter setting a stack of plain paper with airplane potential on each table and walking out of the room. You now have paper; go forth and figure out how to make an airplane. You now have this information; go forth and figure out what to do with it. It's as if the education program is not

129

responsible for facilitating learning – it's the learner's job to figure it all out after the event.

Attendees may appreciate the paper and file it when back at the office with the PowerPoint slides hoping one day they'll have some time to figure out where the folds go so they can make that paper airplane. But if that is the result of your education programs, that's not learning.

Instead, we should be offering fold by fold experiences. We should prototype our paper airplanes together, test how different folds result in different flight arcs, and debrief: *How could you use airplanes like this? What modifications might you make? When do you think you'll implement this new airplane-folding methodology within your context of practice?* Also, send home transformational tools that reinforce what we've learned and recommend additional resources and courses you offer to continue mastering this craft.

To maintain your competitive advantage, become the organization that not only provides the paper and folding techniques, but offers pathways to folding mastery. Show the way. Be the way.

Red Light, Green Light

If you scored green on the Learning Design Drivers, you're in the choir hearing me preach and know beyond doubt this is a significant differentiator sealing your competitive advantage.

If you scored yellow, I'm excited by your curiosity and cursory commitment to step into this space. You have likely experienced some early wins piloting programs that have been designed with intention and witnessed the remarkable difference that investment makes. So exciting! Continue this good work introducing learning design best practices to each program in your portfolio.

If you scored red in this segment of the Scorecard, you now have the advantage of knowing what to do about it. If you're willing to commit to one driver in this segment, commit to the first. Decide how instructional design will inform the choices you make for your education programs. Will you invest in hiring instructional designers? Will you provide memberships to your education team to the Association for Talent Development and send them to the learning design courses for professional development? Or will you pull in contract talent, whether my team or others, to collaborate with you on designing programs that result in transformation? Align resources with this priority, because it is the rocket fuel to your competitive advantage.

Competitive Advantage

Learning design is not an accessory; it is core to your competitive advantage. Learning design undergirds your value proposition – meaningful and measurable results– which is critical to your market positioning and program profitability. Learning design is the differentiator in your market and the difference you can make in the lives of the professionals you represent.

The value proposition in continuing education is *transformation*. Learning design reliably delivers this. So the question is, do you want to deliver this? Do you want to be the go-to source for learning that makes a difference in lives, that elevates the profession, that cements your competitive advantage?

Because if you do, learning design must become a strategic priority. Presently, it's in the blind spot of many organizations that are marketing continuing education. It's time to invite learning design to the party to transform our continuing education business and the lives we touch.

Chapter 9:

Pivot Pain

*"We cannot become what we want
by remaining what we are."*

MAX DUPREE

Resistance Default

As you made your way through the book to this point, perhaps highlighting some sections, selecting ratings on the drivers and capturing notes on next steps, pause also to note any areas where you felt resistance.

When clients invite me to deliver a strategy session, whether on the full Scorecard or a component of it, I have trained my ear to hear discomfort and doubt. Because they've invited me, and because I've vetted them for readiness, I know they really want to embrace change and innovate. As I facilitate discussion, I bring forward the points of discomfort and resistance I hear so we can excavate where the seed issue lies and determine whether that issue will disrupt our implementation and sustainability.

Discomfort or the questions bubbling up from doubt do not mean the concept is wrong or even that you shouldn't do it. Those feelings mean there's something more to examine. Take the challenge. Identify items that caused you to give me side-eye and pause now to ask yourself the 5 Whys. Simply articulate why you feel discomfort with the idea, ask yourself why that is, record the answer, and then ask yourself why again – five times. At the end of your excavation, see whether you truly have an immovable obstacle or a belief that needs to be shifted.

Sit with the knowing we cannot continue to do the same things and expect different results. We cannot copy/paste quick fixes and expect sustainable ROI. We cannot expect outdated models to propel us into profitability when we see declining membership, registration and revenue threats across industries.

What resistance defaults are keeping you where you are? Here are some of the obstacles I commonly hear.

Common External Factors

It's easy to blame the environment and external forces that keep us pinned in place. We tell ourselves we can't do anything about it. That's just the way it is.

The first common factor is blaming members. Members like things the way they are – they prefer lecture formats and don't want to interact. Members don't like change. Members won't work with us to try learning formats or respond fondly to speaker accountability. They're just used to our conference and the way we allow them to choose all the session topics for the program. They know best. This is their association.

For member-based organizations, it's an easy out to say members will or members won't. And we may even frame that in terms of serving our members' needs and desires for their professional association. But when thinking like a business, it suddenly becomes silly to say, *Customers like our twenty-year-old menu the way it is – they prefer our age-old recipes and don't want to try eating local, fresh ingredients. They don't like quinoa. They don't want what's good for them. And they're our customer so they know best.*

Do members actually prefer lecture? Or are they accustomed to our menu? Do they really dislike interaction, or are they wise to the annoying use of ice breakers masquerading as engagement? Are you certain speakers will not work with you to improve the learning experience? Or does it just feel hard to ask?

The second common factor is blaming leaders. The board members or board chair or committee members just don't value this. They don't understand why we would need to invest in learning design. They like the prestige of making content decisions about events. We might be able to put on some enhancements, but our leaders just want things the way they want them.

If the leadership is truly informed, why wouldn't they value seizing the competitive advantage? Do they have all the information available before making the decision to cripple your profitability and sustainability? Also, much of what we chat about in the Scorecard are business decisions. The senior staff leadership is responsible to the organization for sound business decision-making. This isn't a choice between the LMS with bells or the one with whistles. This is about a business model that will ensure your survival. I think they can probably get behind that. It's worth investigating the root of the resistance here.

The third common factor is blaming regulation. Our programs must be boring, long lecture-lands because of legislation, compliance, the new rule, liability, accreditation standards, etc. I've worked in regulated industries, and I've experienced the challenges of navigating these structures. None of them prohibit us from developing a strategy, managing our portfolio effectively, or designing learning experiences that pave the way to mastery. If compliance programs are *not* designed for transformation, there is no reason to expect behavior to change. Regulation paints some boundaries on our playing court, but they don't take away our game.

While the blame game is common, the problem is rarely who or what is being blamed. It's often fear of change or anxiety around taking responsibility to address the conditions. I'm a big fan of incremental innovations because making even small changes can significantly shift our environment.

Quick story: Several years ago, I went on a camping and climbing trip with friends on the North Shore. I was there for the hiking and camping part, having never climbed before, but was somehow talked into trying it. I got my permit and put on some borrowed equipment as my friends tied me in. I stood at the top of the route on Shovel Point looking down, my heart racing as they quickly explained how this was going to work. I would step off the side of the rock cliff and rappel down a good length. Not all the way down where Lake Superior was crashing against the rock – just a good length. And then, climb up.

It seemed simple enough.

The route is called "Out on a Limb."

I reached a footing my fellow climbers thought would be a good starting point for me and promptly freaked out. Turns out, it was almost sheer! I hung there for a while searching for hand and foot holds. How was I going to scale this thing? Down was not an option. And at the moment, up didn't seem like a great option either. But I knew that staying put was also not going to work, so I found a hold. I shifted my weight so I could stick my shoe and move upward to a better foothold. And then, just like my climbing pro friends told me, a whole new array of options became available.

That insight revolutionized my climb. I realized that from one point of view the rock face looked completely sheer, but just a small shift in holds revealed the next best option to me.

As you likely guessed, I made it to the top. It was hard and scary and exhausting and exhilarating. I realized I could do things I believed I could not do. I left Tettagouche knowing my strength and resourcefulness is deeper and wider than I perceived. And I've taken that lesson with me into business and life.

Don't blame the rock face for being sheer. Stick your shoe. Shift your foothold. Notice what additional options come into view after implementing your incremental innovations.

Common Internal Factors

Internal factors can seem even more insurmountable. I've heard many, but here are the top five.

The first is lack of budget. We don't have money to experiment with our conference, license an LMS, invest in learning design, or hire the right talent to move our objectives forward. We want to innovate, but we don't want to invest in innovating.

Money is real, and managing budgets is typically a requirement to remain employed. The question is, when you look at the budget, is it aligned with your strategic objectives? Are there things you're paying for that you really don't need or don't serve the organization any longer? Are there programs that need to be cut but haven't because someone has announced them sacred and untouchable? Where might you free up some of what you need from corners of the budget where money is stuck but not serving you well?

If you and your partner decided you wanted to road trip from Lake Itasca where the Mississippi is born to where it flows into the Gulf of Mexico and you knew in your hearts that for you the only way to fulfill this dream was with a T@B S teardrop camper with interior kitchen and wet bath, how would you come up with that $25,000? Would you figure since that money isn't in the bank, it's pointless, or would you look for options like seasonal work, selling the motorcycle, cutting back on some expenses, making room in the budget for making your dream come true? No, a camper is not the same as contracting a learning designer, but the concepts of finding room for what you want to see happen is pretty much the same. If it's a priority, you'll find a way.

The second internal factor is lack of staff. I work with organizations that have two staff and organizations with hundreds. Organizations of all sizes say this. But what does it really mean? Does it mean all of the staff are already aligned with executing strategic objectives (education and otherwise), all workflows are optimized, volunteer management is efficient and effective, and we don't suffer technology work-arounds but fix issues – but we just don't have enough people? Or does it mean we feel tapped and thinking about doing more makes us tired? Talent management can be a tough conversation for an organization. But challenge the assumption that you don't have enough staff to cut back dead wood projects and innovate for your organization's competitive advantage.

Lack of confidence is the third factor. I see this manifest in a couple ways. The first is leaders who are overwhelmed with the options and the risk of making a poor or uninformed choice, serving up an amygdala fright freeze. They reach out to me to tell them what to do – they just want to know the right way and for me to give them the answers. This one we can address with some coaching. The second is a deeper concern: lack of confidence in execution. These clients reference times when they've tried new ideas but implementation fell apart or the innovation just didn't stick, and they reverted backward.

This requires deeper work getting to the why, but it's a hurdle we can hop to ensure sustainability.

A fourth factor is lack of support. This may manifest on the leadership level or the peer-collaboration level. And because we need top-down and sideways commitment to implement transformational learning, the Scorecard requires we start at the top with our strategic objectives and leadership level commitments. It requires that we be accountable for how we work together to manage a portfolio of learning and collaborate across divisions. This alignment should be cloned in all divisions, setting you up as a high-functioning organization prepared to powerfully serve its members. And this is another reason I am advocating that this is not an event team issue; it's an association management issue. A commitment to support profitable and sustainable transformational learning.

Finally, the fifth factor I hear is lack of time. There's just not enough time to step away and strategize, make plans, implement new things, measure new things, and manage all of this to sustain change.

But you have time to maintain the status quo.

Time isn't a scarce resource; it's a used or misused resource. Asking your 5 Why's will help you uncover why you believe you do not have enough time, and possibly, how your time is presently prioritized. If positioning your organization to make money while making an impact in your industry is priority, you will find the time to make it happen or budget for additional talent.

Each of these blame and lack factors are ultimately perceptions. They are mirages of obstacles with root causes we can address with our incremental innovations. But what if you came to the decision that yes, shifting our momentum now is just too hard. What would staying stuck cost?

Cost of Inaction

In Chapter 1, we talked about complex stratification of the adult education market and the enormous competition we face. We noted the shifting concept of career and the demands professionals face to acquire portable marketable skills. We touched on key trends that are driving the modern learner's expectations for learning at the point of need. Change is our reality. Choosing not to do anything about it is still a choice.

What if we fail?

What if you *succeed*?

Reward	Sacrifice
Now that we're embracing learning design, our transformational learning programs improve our workforce and generate learner loyalty – because their value lies in making a difference in lives.	Pulling down silos and coordinating content means internal "kingdoms" will be disrupted. And it will take effort to get subject experts to work with us differently, too.

Now that we have a three-level evaluation plan, we can measure our success and intervene when issues arise – making intentional gains toward our targets.	It may be a while before we see the results of our efforts. Some volunteer leaders serve so they can advance personal agendas and legacy issues – we'll have to manage all that to maintain commitment to strategic goals and an evaluation plan. We'll have to draw new lines between business decisions and stakeholder decisions.
Now that we've established our strategic objectives and business plan targets, we have established priorities we can follow through on.	This takes time to envision and implement. We're already stretched thin and can barely get our current workload done. Now we must do this, too? We'll have to have some tough conversations about prioritization so we can align resources with the results we want. It won't be popular with some staff or volunteer leaders. We'll have to constructively work through that conflict.
Now that we're clear on our target audiences, how to design to facilitate learning, and how to measure results, we can more effectively market our impact to our learner prospects and to employers.	Changing systems and processes and how we collaborate across teams is hard. This is just not how we do things around here. New systems of accountability will have to be put in place. We'll have to follow through on actually acting on the data we collect.

We are tapped into our marketplace and the needs of our constituencies, so we can position ourselves and differentiate the learning experiences we offer.	This sounds expensive. We'll have to stop relying on the occasional needs survey and committee feedback and do some real research. We may not like some of the answers.
We have engaged a strategic framework that ensures our association's continuing education programs are reliably profitable, sustainable, and make a measurable impact on the industry we represent.	A culture shift will be required. That sounds hard. It will require more than an All-Staff. We'll have to work it into the muscle of our organization, which requires commitment, attention, and time.

Are any of these sacrifices bad? Aren't these things you know you *should* give up to get ahead?

If education is central to your association's mission and value proposition, examine what is preventing you from embracing the opportunity to transform a workforce through your continuing education programming. What is preventing you from becoming the go-to learning leader?

The cost of indecision is staying put while the CE market settles a new planet.

Board the rocket with me.

Chapter 10:
Strategy to Action

"Most people will talk the talk, few will walk the walk. Be among the few."

DR. STEVE MARABOLI, UNAPOLOGETICALLY YOU

Liftoff

I vividly remember taking centering breaths as the elevator descended to the lobby. My shoes clicked on the immaculate marble tile floors. Honestly, I felt like I was going to throw up. I was a seasoned professional but new to this association. I was tasked with a high-profile initiative – to create a complex online performance improvement program that would meet maintenance of certification (MOC) requirements and be a meaningful experience for our members. The association had already taken one running start at this without success, so this second attempt had to be a winner.

I spotted the physician editor I had been collaborating with and joined him for a quick debrief on our presentation before we stepped into the joint committee meeting. His laid-back Northern California energy put me at ease. He expressed confidence in the work we had done – deep listening, comprehensive market scanning, and a digital framework that was the simplest solution we could offer within our desired timeframe. He was right. Our rationale was sound. Our solution wasn't perfect but darn good. If our presentation was just being judged on facts, we were super solid. But the roiling in my gut was more so in anticipation of the emotional charge around the MOC program. MOC was born out of complex political and public pressure to increase accountability in medical practice and decrease medical error – preventable adverse effects of care. So there are reasonably a lot of strong feelings about this on all sides. And there our learning program initiative lay in the middle of all the rocks and hard places.

Turns out the presentation went very well. We laid a strategic foundation that won leadership buy-in. So we set to work: collaborating across organization silos, architecting a custom technology infrastructure, and bringing forward best practices in behavior change learning design to the experience. I was in my family room late at night several months later wrapping up QA on our first module. And then I realized *it was done*. All the development and figuring out how reality fits into best-laid plans and collaborating with our faculty to create something they had no way of seeing because they were *creating* the prototype – we did it. I texted my editor, *It's ready. Go for launch?*

He replied, *Do it.*

And we went live.

Did execution go 100 percent smoothly? No, it did not. It was downright painful at times because we had to internally disrupt how we were accustomed to owning projects to embrace a collaborative teaming model. We had to work with faculty who could not see or touch the final product while developing the content – which is a tough ask. We were collaborating with our crack digital team testing software as they developed it while concurrently preparing the learning resources it would soon feature. It was a lot. We had to learn how to do this as we did this, iterating on the fly.

But were we successful in achieving our launch goals? Yes! As one of my staff colleagues noted, we created something out of nothing – bridging a concept to a strategy to action. An incredible feat for the entire team. And I am so impressed with this organization's gumption acknowledging that yep, it will be uncomfortable and different working this way, but it's a priority. So figure it out.

All that to say this book isn't pie in the sky. I know what I'm asking of you. I work in those same trenches, and I've felt the pressures. I have also witnessed what's possible. I share this product launch experience as a microcosm example. We had to build our strategic foundation and design a path forward within the boundaries of our resources. We had to create new ways to collaborate internally – both as a cross-functional team and as a learning program that curated assets from other sources within the association's portfolio. And from the first moment, we were dedicated to learning design, building an experience that would be meaningful and make a measurable difference (we actually measured!). And because we accomplished this together, we now knew so much more was possible. Yes, there were thoughtful plans and there were also emotions and personal stakes and weird budgeting gymnastics to pool shared resources. But once you've shifted your footing and you see that new handholds do become available, you begin to trust it. And then you realize things you thought were impossible are the first step toward what's next.

Become the Disruptor

The way we do business in the continuing education market has been disrupted. The way professionals develop their careers and access learning resources has been disrupted. To meet these conditions, we must disrupt our status quo.

I challenge you: Become the disruptor.

Become the organization that sets its strategic goal sites and aligns resources to meet them – creating a runway to reliable profit.

Become the organization that maximizes its entire learning portfolio to meet market needs while raising the bar on team collaboration and efficiencies – initiating practices that produce sustainability.

Become the organization dedicated to learner transformation vital to workforce development – driving measurable impact.

Begin where you are. You've got this!

Education Enterprise Scorecard Drivers

You now have a tool to navigate the conversations required to become reliably profitable, sustainable through impactful continuing education. You've now worked through the Scorecard, rating your organization on each driver so you can assess where to prioritize focus. These drivers are the levers in your continuing education business. Adjustments will impact your system. I recommend benchmarking where you are today and returning to the Scorecard to view your progress and new areas of focus as you refine your practice.

For quick-scan review, our Scorecard drivers are as follows:

Strategy

1. Market Intelligence
2. Strategic Objectives
3. Target Audience(s)
4. Content Priorities
5. Program Pricing
6. Technology Infrastructure
7. Internal Partnerships
8. External Partnerships
9. Resource Allocation
10. Evaluation Strategy

Portfolio Management

1. Business Plan
2. Portfolio Evaluation Plan
3. Program Policies

4. Learning Environment
5. Content Calendar
6. Learning Pathways
7. Education Technology Management
8. Customer Service

Learning Design

1. Instructional Design
2. Competency Development
3. Learning Evaluation
4. Design Process
5. Transformational Learning Tools
6. Visual Design
7. SME Development

Still not sure where to begin? Consider the framework below.

Quick-Start Guide

The Education Enterprise Scorecard reveals a powerful approach to building business around continuing education. Your learning portfolio is like a child's mobile – when you tug one of the elephants all the others respond. So it's important to thoughtfully consider your entry point.

If you rated your organization yellow or red on the first four drivers, that's your place to start. Get a handle on your market, even if your first stab is a hearty web search and conversation with your Education Committee. You can't develop an effective strategy unless you know what you're positioning against in your market. This helps you craft a killer value proposition and differentiate your offerings from others.

Next, spend some time developing your strategic objectives. Reflect, brainstorm, and collaboratively refine your organization's list of outcomes for the learning portfolio. As you add an objective to the list, always ask: How will we measure our progress and our fulfilment? Because goals are meaningless without measurement and accountability.

I guarantee it will be difficult to conduct market research or define your strategic objectives without talking about your target audiences. Naturally, you may have objectives more general in scope and some that reference specific audience segments. Just allow that to happen while noting your various constituencies so you can continue the conversation about what each needs from you and what needs you are committed to delivering.

Then take some time to identify your content priorities. I've offered you a process to facilitate a conversation defining your content sandbox and identifying priorities for the coming year. Use these priorities in your calls for proposals. Use these priorities to invite experts to teach. Use these priorities to develop learning pathways and curriculum offering opportunities for mastery.

With these first four drivers in place, the next set of strategy drivers will more easily fall into alignment. Then you can begin working on your business and implementation plans, including how your team and portfolio of learning options will collaborate.

All of this is nice and will improve your sustainability, but without learning design, the competitive struggle will continue. Learning design is your linchpin. It's your market differentiator elevating your value proposition among your competitors. It's the reason you would even care to develop learning pathways supporting the entire learning cycle. It's how your programs pivot from informational to transformational. Learners have access to a lot of information. What they want are results. And we can reliably offer those results by employing learning design.

Why 90 Percent of Organizations' Strategies Fail

Brightline Initiative released a report[12] in 2017 based on a survey of five hundred senior executives of large companies with revenue in the billions. One in ten admit their organization does not deliver all their strategic initiatives successfully. Nearly 60% confess it's a struggle to implement strategy in the organization's day-to-day operations. This is a legitimate issue that even billion-dollar corporations wrestle with. Brightline reports the gap between strategy design and strategy delivery is widening. Organizations who master implementation and cross-function collaboration differentiate themselves from their competition. Strategy documents that get filed are of no value. Our strategy must be evolving and responsive, driven by metrics, accountability, and communication loops connecting the dots of intention with execution. For my clients, whether doing this work for the first time or refining their education strategy, they accelerate with greater confidence because of our coaching and collaboration.

Because this isn't a duct tape quick fix. To offer transformation, we must transform ourselves.

Join me in becoming the disruptor. Because workforce development matters. Because professional associations matter. Because education is intended to be transformational, not transactional. Because we can do better, and now, you know the way, too.

Acknowledgments

This book was born in the trenches where smart, passionate, and dedicated pros labor over how to do this continuing ed thing better. It was inspired by so many conversations, vent sessions, burnout calls for help from colleagues that this is too big to tackle. I survey the CE landscape, helicopter into the canyon, and ride those rapids alongside you. Doing so, I felt compelled to find a better way not just for me, but so we can all rise together.

I have so much gratitude for this journey and the beloved people who have propped me up along the way with their encouragement, great questions, and unwavering support.

Thank you, Mamasita! You have always believed in me – on great days and do-over days. You really see me and my heart. I treasure our bond.

Thanks, Dad! I love that we share a passion for writing, and I especially loved the look on your face when I told you I was writing this book.

Special thanks to my DELP family and for ASAE and the Detroit Metro CVB for investing in the truth that diversity in leadership produces strategic advantages. Particular thanks to the courageous, ambitious, and ridiculously amazing class of 2013–2015 (best class ever!). I'm so inspired by you! Leaders need a fam where they get real and bare their vulnerabilities. And get called out should the occasion arise! I'm so lucky to have you in my life.

Gratitude to Todd Mann for your mentorship and unfailing belief in me, nudging me to trust my gut and go for it. I appreciate your early feedback on the Scorecard back in its infancy. I miss your face!

To the Morgan James Publishing team: Special thanks to David Hancock, CEO & Founder for believing in me and my message. To my Author Relations Manager, Bonnie Rauch, thanks for making the process seamless and easy. Many more thanks to everyone else, but especially Jim Howard, Bethany Marshall, and Nickcole Watkins.

InspirEd continues to grow and flourish, exceeding all my expectations. I'm deeply grateful to my clients – current, past, and future. Clients worth celebrating! Your accomplishments make me proud. Your commitment to step out and stand out are both the impetus for bringing us together and the reason you will continue to expand your competitive advantage. Hugs and high fives to my team for their extraordinary brains, deep servant hearts, and unquenchable curiosity to keep learning and growing. Best team on earth!

Mo – Broders on me!

Thank You!

Thank you for reading *Competitive Advantage*. It's time to become the profitable and sustainable learning authority you know you can be – leaving a magnificent legacy on the industry your organization represents.

I designed the Education Enterprise Scorecard to not only be an assessment tool, but a benchmark capturing progress year over year. As you know, developing a strategy and implementing it isn't once and done. Conditions shift, new priorities emerge, and implementing change can surface new challenges and opportunities. The Scorecard serves as a touchstone ensuring the learning portfolio is functioning at its best.

Until now, I've only offered the Scorecard to my clients. As my thank you, you can grab your own copy of the tool summarizing the twenty-five drivers by visiting www.competitiveadvantagebook.com.

By reading *Competitive Advantage*, some of you now have what you need to draft your education strategy and next steps. Others will feel inspired too, but view this book as the start of a conversation you'd like to take deeper. I'd be honored to connect with you about your competitive advantage. You can reach me to coordinate a strategy session call at tracy@inspired-ed.com or through the InspirEd website www.inspired-ed.com.

Love, light, and learning,
Tracy

About the Author

Tracy King, MA, CAE
CEO and Chief Learning Strategist, InspirEd

Every job Tracy has held contained a training component – it's a fish and water thing. She's designed corporate training, served as academic faculty, and now consults on workforce development, primarily serving professional associations and continuing education organizations. She's a learning strategist, facilitator, and master instructional designer.

Tracy's in-the-trenches experience inspires her drive to research the intersection of learning science and technology. She's a thought leader who breaks down the science into strategies that work. She has developed models for learning design and learner engagement, as well as the Education

Enterprise Scorecard benchmarking the twenty-five drivers for profitable, sustainable, and impactful continuing education.

Tracy has a master's degree in communication; she taught communication theory and public speech at multiple academic centers to students around the world. She is an experienced speech coach and is now an invited speaker on continuing education strategy and learning design.

Complementing her own study of the learning sciences, Tracy has been mentored by neuroscientists in NeuroEducation and has worked alongside them applying those best practices in designing cutting-edge online continuing medical education programs. The programs Tracy has established feature a variety of learning formats from live forums and workshops to digital self-assessment, performance improvement, and interactive multimedia education. Her programs routinely receive high ratings and defy industry completion rate standards.

Tracy is a Certified Association Executive (CAE), the highest credential in nonprofit organization management. This mark of distinction is held by less than 5 percent of all association professionals. She also holds the CVEP credential acknowledging expertise in virtual, hybrid, and online learning and is certified in the Kirkpatrick Four Levels® of learning evaluation.

In recognition of her expertise as a leader and innovator in the association profession, Tracy was selected as an ASAE Diversity Executive Leadership Program (DELP) Scholar. She also served on the ASAE Professional Development Section

Council, which promotes leading-edge practices in adult continuing education, and was the 2015 Council Chair.

Tracy enjoys travel and is amused when people stop and ask her directions as if she's a local in cities she's visiting (this happens a lot!). She's a fan of taste testing regional craft brews. And as a Great Lakes native, she loves the stunning Lake Michigan and Superior landscapes, such as the Apostle Islands, third coast beaches, Leelanau Peninsula vineyards, North Shore waterfalls, and the Lake Superior ice caves. Tracy lives in Minneapolis, the mother bear of four children, two rescue pups, and a cat ghost.

Website: www.inspired-ed.com
Blog: www.tracy-king.com
Email: tracy@inspired-ed.com
Facebook: www.facebook.com/TracyKing.InspirEd/

Endnotes

1 Nabila Amarsy. "How to Scan Your Business Model Environment for Disruptive Threats and Opportunities." Strategyzer. October 15, 2015. http://blog.strategyzer. com/posts/2015/10/14/how-to-scan-through-your-environments-disruptive-threats-and-opportunities

2 "2018 Global Human Capital Trends." Deloitte Insights. https://www2.deloitte.com/insights/us/en/focus/ human-capital-trends.html

3 "Contingent Workforce: Size, Characteristics, Earnings, and Benefits." U.S. Government Accountability Office. April 20, 2015. https://www.gao.gov/assets/670/669899. pdf

4 "Half of Millennials Have a Side Hustle." New York Post. November 14, 2017. https://nypost.com/2017/11/14/ half-of-millennials-have-a-side-hustle/

5 "Bridging the Soft Skills Gap: How the Business and Education Sectors are Partnering to Prepare Students for the 21st Century Workforce." US Chamber of Commerce Foundation. November 6, 2017. https:// www.uschamberfoundation.org/reports/soft-skills-gap

6 "Size of the Training Industry." Training Industry. April 20, 2017.

7 "State of the Industry." ATD Research. December 2017. https://www.td.org/research-reports/2017-state-of-the-industry

8 "Association Learning + Technology Report." Tagoras. 2017. https://www.tagoras.com/catalog/association-learning-technology/

9 Graham Kenny. "Your Strategic Plans Probably Aren't Strategic, or Even Plans." Harvard Business Review. April 6, 2018. https://hbr.org/2018/04/your-strategic-plans-probably-arent-strategic-or-even-plans

10 Will Thalheimer. Performance Focused Smile Sheets: A Radical Rethinking of a Dangerous Art Form. (Work-Learning Press, 2016).

11 James D. and Wendy Kayser Kirkpatrick. Kirkpatrick's Four Levels of Training Evaluation. (Alexandria, VA: ATD Press, 2016).

12 "Closing the Gap: Designing and Delivering Strategy That Works." Brightline Initiative. October 3, 2107. https://www.brightline.org/resources/eiu-report/

CPSIA information can be obtained
at www.ICGtesting.com
Printed in the USA
BVHW081115240919
559260BV00001B/158/P

9 781642 793680